Andreas Berg-Hildebrand / Christian Suhm (Eds.)
Bas C. van Fraassen

9. Münstersche Vorlesungen zur Philosophie 2005
9th Münster Lectures on Philosophy 2005

mit / with

Bas C. van Fraassen

Andreas Berg-Hildebrand
Christian Suhm (Eds.)

Bas C. van Fraassen

The Fortunes of Empiricism

ontos
verlag
Frankfurt | Paris | Ebikon | Lancaster | New Brunswick

Bibliographic information published by Die Deutsche Bibliothek
Die Deutsche Bibliothek lists this publication in the Deutsche Nationalbibliographie; detailed bibliographic data is available in the Internet at http://dnb.ddb.de

transaction

North and South America by
Transaction Books
Rutgers University
Piscataway, NJ 08854-8042
trans@transactionpub.com

Gazelle

United Kingdom, Ire Iceland, Turkey, Malta, Portugal by
Gazelle Books Services Limited
White Cross Mills
Hightown
LANCASTER, LA1 4XS
sales@gazellebooks.co.uk

Livraison pour la France et la Belgique:
Librairie Philosophique J.Vrin
6, place de la Sorbonne ; F-75005 PARIS
Tel. +33 (0)1 43 54 03 47 ; Fax +33 (0)1 43 54 48 18
www.vrin.fr

P. O. Box 15 41, D-63133 Heusenstamm nr. Frankfurt
Tel. ++(49) 6104 66 57 33 Fax ++(49) 6104 66 57 34
www.ontosverlag.com

ISBN 3-938793-14-7

2006

Printed on acid-free paper
ISO-Norm 970-6
FSC-certified (Forest Stewardship Council)

Printed in Germany
by buch bücher **dd ag**

CONTENTS

Preface

Bas C. van Fraassen is among the most distinguished and celebrated philosophers of science of our days. His fields of expertise range from logic and semantics to epistemology and philosophy of physics. Several of his monographs belong to the standard literature of these disciplines. It was already in 1980 when his *The Scientific Image* brilliantly entered the philosophical scene. Especially the exposition of constructive empiricism, van Fraassen's favored philosophy of science as well as his alternative to scientific realism, launched an intensive and highly controversial debate on the aim and status of science which has not at all been settled up to now.

In his Terry Lectures at Yale University (published as *The Empirical Stance* in 2002) Bas van Fraassen gave a comprehensive account of what he deems to be cogent answers to the questions of what empiricism is and what it could be. In due distance to the self-defeating fundamentalist projects of logical empiricism he envisaged empiricism as a stance, as opposed to a factual thesis. From his point of view it is the recurrent rebellion against metaphysics and the admiration for science that characterizes the empiricists' stance and buttresses their philosophical arguments. It is beyond doubt that the prospects of empiricism today are intimately related to Bas van Fraassen and his work.

The Department of Philosophy at the University of Münster invited Bas van Fraassen to the *10. Münstersche Vorlesungen zur Philosophie.* He gave a lecture to a public audience on the 30th of May 2005 titled "Weyl's Paradox: The Distance Between Structure and Perspective". Papers on his philosophy, which were written by students and faculty of the Department of Philosophy, were intensively discussed on the following two days. Both the lecture and the papers are published in revised form in this volume. In addition, it contains detailed replies to the colloquium papers by Bas van Fraassen.

First of all, our deep and warm thanks go to Bas van Fraassen. We owe him much gratitude for his lecture, for his participation in the colloquium, and his extensive replies to the papers. It was an intriguing experience for all participants of the colloquium to discuss his philosophy with him and to learn from his instructive and subtle responses. We could not have wished for a kinder and more patient partner in discussion.

We would like to thank all students and colleagues of the Department of Philosophy for the preparation of the colloquium papers and for their various contributions to the discussion. We could not have realized this volume without their excellent cooperation and help. We are also very grateful to David P. Schweikard for revising the papers.

On behalf of the Department of Philosophy we express our sincere thankfulness to the ontos verlag for generously funding the series of the *Münstersche Vorlesungen zur Philosophie* and for making this publication possible.

Münster, April 2006 *Andreas Berg-Hildebrand, Christian Suhm*

List of Abbreviations of Bas C. van Fraassen's Publications

ACE	"Armstrong, Cartwright, and Earman on Laws and Symmetry", *Philosophy and Phenomenological Research* LIII, pp. 431-444, 1999.
CEMN	"Constructive Empiricism and Modal Nominalism", (with Bradley Monton), *British Journal for the Philosophy of Science*, 54, pp. 405-422, 2003.
CEN	"Constructive Empiricism Now", *Philosophical Studies* 106. pp. 151-170, 2001.
EPS	"Empiricism in the philosophy of science", in P.M. Churchland and C.A.Hooker (eds.): *Images of Science: Essays on Realism and Empiricism, with a Reply by Bas C. van Fraassen.* Chicago: University of Chicago Press, pp. 245-308, 1985.
ES	*The Empirical Stance.* Yale: Yale University Press 2002.
FHTE	"The False Hopes of Traditional Epistemology", *Philosophy and Phenomenological Research* 60, pp. 253-280, 2000.
GRCE	"Gideon Rosen on Constructive Empiricism", *Philosophical Studies* 74, pp. 179-192, 1994.
LE	"Literate Experience: The [De-, Re-] Interpretation of Nature", *Versus* 85/86/87, pp. 331-358, 2002.
LS	*Laws and Symmetry.* Oxford: Oxford University Press 1989.
MM	"On McMullin's Appreciation of Realism Concerning the Sciences", *Philosophy of Science* 70, pp. 479-492, 2003.
MRAP	"Meaning Relations Among Predicates", *Nous* l, pp. 160-179, 1967.
MRM	"Meaning Relations and Modalities", *Nous* 3, pp. 155-167, 1969.
ONVN	"The only necessity is verbal necessity", *Journal of Philosophy* 74, pp. 71-85, 1977.

OQI "On the Question of Identification of a Scientific Theory (A Reply To "Van Fraassens Concept Of Empirical Theory" By Pérez Ransanz)", *Critica* 17, pp. 21-25, 1985.

PLS "Précis of *Laws and Symmetry*", *Philosophy and Phenomenological Research* LIII, pp. 411-412, 1993.

PP "Putnam's Paradox: Metaphysical Realism Revamped And Evaded", *Philosophical Perspectives* 11, Boston: Blackwell, pp. 17-42, 1997.

RDES "Replies to Discussion on *The Empirical Stance*", *Philosophical Studies* 121, pp. 171-192, 2004.

RPS "Representation: the Problem for Structuralism", *PSA* 2004 proceedings, forthcoming in *Philosophy of Science.*

SAST "The Semantic Approach to Scientific Theories", in Nancy J. Nersessian (ed.): *The Process of Science.* Dordrecht: Kluwer, pp. 105-124, 1987.

SI *The Scientific Image.* Oxford: Oxford University Press 1980.

SP "Structure and Perspective: Philosophical Perplexity and Paradox", in M.L. Dalla Chiara et al. (eds.): *Logic and Scientific Methods.* Dordrecht: Kluwer, pp. 511-530, 1997.

VC "From Vicious Circle to Infinite Regress, and Back Again", in D. Hull, M. Forbes, and K. Ohkruhlik (eds.): *PSA* 1992, Vol. 2. Evanston: Northwestern University Press, pp. 6-29, 1993.

WE "The World of Empiricism", in J. Hilgevoort (ed.): *Physics and Our View of the World.* Cambridge (Mass.), pp. 114-134, 1994.

WIBL "Wouldn't It Be Lovely?". Review of P. Lipton, *Inference to the Best Explanation* (2nd ed.), *Metascience* 14, pp. 344-352, 2005.

WEYL'S PARADOX: THE DISTANCE BETWEEN STRUCTURE AND PERSPECTIVE

Bas C. van Fraassen

In the decades just before and after 1900 the arguments engaged in by scientists and philosophers in Germany, France, and Britain concerned not only the directions that science should take but also the very idea of what science was or was to be. My interest in their arguments is certainly anachronistic: I see them as pertaining to issues central to our conception of science today, and as pointing out problems that we must face in our own way, but helped greatly by how they confronted similar problems then.

1 Science as Representation

Here is at least a partial truth: Science is a representation, of the observable phenomena, by means of mathematical models. I say partial, because I am taking science here not in the sense of the ongoing activity that we call science, but its products received both within and outside of the scientific community. These products include many concrete representations – models that can be displayed on table tops or computer monitors – but in the end have to be developed in mathematics, simply because neither the infinitesimal nor the infinite can be so displayed. From this truth about what science gives us, I will draw two consequences.

Consequence 1: Science represents structure only. The book of science is written in the language of mathematics, and mathematics represents structure alone.

Consequence 2: Science is essentially perspectival; we cannot understand what it does except in relation to us, the doers.

1.1 Weyl on isomorphism

> A science can never determine its subject-matter except up to isomorphic representation. The idea of isomorphism indicates the self-understood, insurmountable barrier of knowledge. [...] [T]oward the "nature" of its objects science maintains complete indifference. This – for example what distinguishes the colors from the points of the projective plane – one can only *know* in immediate alive intuition.[1]

Weyl thus accompanies the point about this limitation with an immediate recognition of the 'something else' which is then left un-represented. When two objects are represented by isomorphic structures – hence, when their representation presents no difference between them – we may still know that they are *distinct* and in un-represented ways *different* objects. This sounds paradoxical, it tends to suggest the following equally unpalatable alternatives:

- that either the point about isomorphism and mathematics is mistaken, or
- that scientific representation is not at bottom mathematical representation alone, or
- that science is necessarily incomplete in a way we can know it to be, or
- that those apparent differences to us are illusory.

Weyl appears to opt for the second, or perhaps the third, alternative. But on either, we face here a perplexing epistemological question:

1 Weyl (1934), p. 19.

Is there something that I could know to be the case, and which is not expressed by a proposition that could be part of some scientific theory?

This question we will pursue, and return to explicitly at the end.

1.2 The history behind Weyl's point

When non Euclidean geometries were first created, the question arose whether there could be an empirical test to decide whether space is Euclidean. In principle it seemed easy enough. For example, in Euclidean space the interior angles of a triangle add up to 180 degrees. In hyperbolic geometry it is not so. Gauss' earlier studies of surfaces with negative curvature could be applied here. In a three-sided figure whose sides are arcs of minimal length, the interior angles sum to less than 180 degrees, the defect increasing with the area. But the extent of this defect depends on the curvature of the surface, which may be very small in which case the differences from a surface of zero curvature (Euclidean plane) would show up significantly only in very large areas.

Lobachevsky measures

So Lobachevsky looked into astronomical data. He suggested that one might "investigate a stellar triangle for an experimental resolution of the question." The "stellar triangle" he proposed was the star Sirius and two different positions of the Earth at 6-month intervals. But if there was such a defect in the sum of the interior angles, it was still within the limits of measurement error.

Indeed, for any defect you can name and any size, there would be a curvature constant small enough to guarantee that the defect would still be within those limits. So, if there are also limits on the size of the regions we can inspect in this way in the course of human history, the difference between Euclidean and hyperbolic space may be beyond what such measurements can reveal.

Helmholtz

But there is a deeper problem. The measurement results will also depend on what we take as measurement standard, and what presuppositions are in place with that choice. This point can be graphically (though only imperfectly) illustrated by v. Helmholtz's examples of mirror-universes. Helmholtz imagined that we are making measurements to determine whether our space is Euclidean. Do the interior angles of a triangle add up to 180 degrees? Suppose they do. At the same time he imagines that we are reflected in a huge concave mirror.

In that mirror we see little people moving around with rulers and 'doing the same thing' as we do. Of course, they get the 'same' results, and announce that they live in a Euclidean space. We want to disagree; they are moving around on a concave surface, and their measuring rods change length as they work.

> All geometrical measurements [...] with regularly varying images of real instruments would yield exactly the same results as in the outer world [...]. I do not see how men in the mirror are to discover [the in-] correctness of Euclid's axioms.[2]

Notice how this relates to Weyl's point. The reflection in the mirror is a perfect image of what is reflected. If we do not look at any relation of these two sides to ourselves (or any third object or background in which they are located) then they have precisely the same structure. Thus this example illustrates an isomorphism. Two objects which are isomorphic are mathematically no different from each other. We my overlook this if we, very naturally, think of the two as parts of a larger structure (or as related to ourselves as onlookers). In that larger context such parts may indeed be distinguishable, namely by their relations to other parts or to the whole. But if we are dealing with the world as a whole and a model of the world – as in a theory of physical space – then we have no such recourse.

2 Helmholtz (1956), p. 661.

Mathematicians' reaction[3]

One response to the birth of non-Euclidean geometry had thus been that the question might be subject to empirical test. This had not fared well. It was by no means the only or even the most acceptable idea about this new subject at the time. Another main reaction was that to understand non-Euclidean geometries they had to be interpreted within Euclidean geometry. To be intelligible they should be readable as strangely worded descriptions of parts or aspects of Euclidean space. That this is possible was shown initially for the hyperbolic plane by Beltrami in his *Saggio di Interpretatione della Geometria Non Euclidia* (1868).[4] Beltrami himself expressed his goal as maintaining Euclidean geometry as the one true theory of space.

Felix Klein perceived the limits of this effort and first attempted to interpret both Euclidean and non Euclidean geometries within projective geometry. But very soon through Klein's work, and even more radically through Riemann's, there came into being such a cornucopia of geometries that any true theory of space underlying all of them could be very little more than pure logic.

The mathematicians' response was that none were privileged, all geometries were on a par and certain to remain parts of mathematics. But how do they relate to the physical world which we investigate empirically? With the focus shifted to interpretation, that problem has now taken on a very different shape. It is no longer a straightforward question that could be settled by measurement.

Klein's idea that a single projective space could be the domain of either a Euclidean or non-Euclidean geometry introduced a new way of viewing the matter. Thus with Klein, and also Lie, we get a different feeling: they display the Euclidean and non-Euclidean geometries as pertaining to a single space,

3 See Torretti (1984), pp. 52, 63-64, 74, 149-152.

4 The result was not perfectly satisfactory. Poincaré's models of the hyperbolic plane (see note below) are considerably more user-friendly. Beltrami himself asserted that no similar interpretation is possible for hyperbolic 3-space in Euclidean 3-space, presumably because he had provided a Euclidean surface extended in three dimensions to model the hyperbolic plane. The model also has singularities, and Hilbert proved later that the hyperbolic plane cannot be mapped isometrically onto a Euclidean surface with no such singularities.

the space of projective geometry, but with different *metrics* – or if you like, different *congruence relations*. Different congruence relations imposed on the same space give it a different geometry.

This ties in well with Helmholtz' illustration: with different measurement techniques, we may be mapping out different congruence relations. To find out whether two different objects are congruent we would presumably do something like this: transport a meter-stick from one to the other. But that we have designated this instrument as a meter-stick, hence as establishing congruence, is a choice, and may have alternatives. Noting then how this ties in with Helmholtz' mirror imaging, and the latter with Weyl's point, we can now see how pervasively Weyl's paradox shows up. The physicist – or more likely, the realist philosopher of science – 'wishes to find out what things are like'. But the mathematician says 'that makes sense only while taking for granted your choices when you accepted or created measurement standards and kept in place a whole host of presuppositions – apart from that, there are no real differences to be found'.

Philosophers' reaction: There must be 'a fact of the matter'!

When Bertrand Russell wrote his *Essay on Geometry* he followed Klein's lead in this reconstruction of the different geometries, which ranged Euclidean and non Euclidean geometries under projective geometry. He even gave what purports to be an a priori, or perhaps transcendental, argument that physical space must be of this sort – in modern terms, this means that physical space must have constant curvature. But Russell added that there must be a unique real relation of congruence.

Given that, it follows that there is a fact of the matter, whether space is really Euclidean or not. Geometry, at least the geometry used in physics, must be according to Russell a non-vacuous theory of real spatial relations.

But how are those real relations identified? Russell maintains that we are directly acquainted with them, through intuition. Having been pressed to elaborate on this view by Poincaré's review in 1899, Russell dismissed the question.[5] That is, he said, like asking me to spell the letter 'A'.

Frege elaborated his similar response in a controversy with Hilbert during the years 1899-1906.[6] The theory of space must be non-vacuous and true. But the question of truth can't arise unless the primitive terms have an independent meaning which fixes their reference. They certainly cannot get that meaning from the axioms or theorems, as Hilbert asserted. For those axioms and theorems are incapable of having a truth value unless their terms have referents. Pressed to explain how we identify those real spatial relations, Frege also retreated to intuition or direct acquaintance: "I give the name of axioms to propositions which are true, but which are not demonstrated, because their knowledge proceeds from a source which is not logical, which we may call space intuition".[7] This was of course just the sort of thing which Poincaré and Hilbert explicitly professed not to understand.

The view that Russell and Frege were resisting may aptly be called *structuralism*, though it is anachronistic to name it thus. They insisted that there was something more to be known, and in fact captured in scientific theories representing nature, than mathematics affords – something more than mathematical structure. Certainly, for the mathematician, all congruence relations, and all possible denotata of their primitive terms, have equal status – but for the empirical sciences there must be more to be known, there must be a fact of the matter that goes beyond what mathematicians can describe.

Presumably in part under pressure from the mathematicians' critique, Russell moved successively farther from this point of view in his subsequent writings, till by his *The Analysis of Matter* (1927) he was espousing a radical structuralism with respect to science, according to which all that science tells us of nature is captured in purely logical/mathematical terms:

5 Poincaré reviewed the book in 1899 and Russell replied. His reply (similar to Frege's point of view, see below, and the discussion in Coffa) is in effect that the axioms of geometry are statements capable of being true or false, which presupposes that their terms designate; what those designata are like determines the truth value. This will later be elaborated e.g. in the still popularly read and used *Problems of Philosophy*: we must be acquainted with all the ultimate constituents of any proposition we understand (hence acquainted with such relations as congruence).

6 See Coffa (1986); Torretti (1984), Ch. 3, section 2.10.

7 In correspondence with Hilbert; quoted Torretti (1984), p. 235.

> [...] whenever we infer from perceptions it is only structure that we can validly infer; and structure is what can be expressed by mathematical logic.
> The only legitimate attitude about the physical world seems to be one of complete agnosticism as regards all but its mathematical properties.[8]

But let us see how the scenario played out further on the Continent meanwhile.

2 Carnap: Der Logische Aufbau der Welt

Carnap published his *Der Logische Aufbau* two years after Russell's *Analysis of Matter*, and begins Part Two with the announcement

> [...] we shall maintain and seek to establish the thesis that science deals only with the description of structural properties of objects.

And he immediately specifies what this will amount to:

> A property description indicates the properties [...], while a relation description [...] does not make any assertion about the objects as individuals.[9]

> There is a certain type of relation description which we shall call *structure description*. Unlike relation descriptions, these not only leave the properties of the individual elements of the range unmentioned, they do not even specify the relations themselves which hold between these elements. In a structure description, only the structure of the relation is indicated, i.e. the totality of its formal properties.[10]

8 Russell (1927), pp. 254, 270.
9 Carnap (1967), section 10, p. 19.
10 Carnap (1967), section 11, p. 21.

2.1 *The crucial problem*

The problem that we started with, using Weyl's words, then appears in the next section:

> Thus, our thesis, namely that scientific statements relate only to structural properties, amounts to the assertion that scientific statements speak only of forms without stating what the elements and the relations of these forms are. Superficially, this seems to be a paradoxical assertion [...] in empirical science, one ought to know whether one speaks of persons or villages. This is the decisive point: *empirical science must be in a position to distinguish these various entities* [...].[11]

Weyl's statement five years later in Philadelphia echoes this point, but Carnap does not seem to have appreciated it so clearly.

How does Carnap deal with this problem? He admits that it *looks as if* the use of definite descriptions will be successful only if eventually it relies on some *ostensive* description – that is, some recourse to pointing or other indexical or demonstrative form of reference. He takes that look to be deceptive:

> However, we shall presently see that, within any object domain, a unique system of definite descriptions is in principle possible, even without the aid of ostensive description.[12]

But his elaboration immediately lets us doubt this irenic assurance:

> It is of especial importance to consider the possibility of such a system for the totality of all objects of knowledge. Even in this case it is not possible to make an a priori decision. But we shall see later that any intersubjective, rational science presupposes this possibility.[13]

11 Carnap (1967), section 12, p. 23.
12 Carnap (1967), pp. 24f.
13 Carnap (1967), p. 25.

What we see here is a vacillation between several possibilities.

(A) Is nature so structured that everything can be uniquely identified by means of a description that captures only that structure?

Carnap has an illustration: the stations in the Eurasian railroad system can be each uniquely identified by listing just the railroad connections between them. But if this system has some global symmetries, then the identifications would not be unique. What if we bring in more structural features, besides the railroad connection relation? Can we be sure that if we bring in enough – when we are at the level of "a system for the totality of all objects of knowledge" we will not be plagued with such non-uniqueness? Here we come to

(B) "any intersubjective, rational science presupposes this possibility".

If that is so we have a transcendental justification for the assertion that knowledge of structure includes all the knowledge there is to be had. Disturbingly, Carnap throws out yet a third option in this Part: that

(C) we should adopt an ontology in which isomorphism implies identity.

Quite a move, for a father of logical positivism and the author of *Pseudoproblems in Philosophy*!

2.2 *Return to the problem*

In Part Four of the *Aufbau* Carnap returns to this problem.[14] He has been envisaging reconstructions of the body of science, or other parts of knowledge, and it seems that he views the structuralist program announced in Part One in the same way as Russell at this point.

14 I want to thank Daniel Rothschild for directing me to this and for much helpful discussion.

> A purely structural statement must contain only logical symbols [...]. Thus [...] the problem arises whether it is possible to complete this formalization by *eliminating from the statements of science these basic relations* [...]. That this elimination is possible becomes obvious [...].[15]

The elimination must replace relation descriptions by structure descriptions, as we saw above, that is to say, by assertions that there are relations having certain properties, and instantiated in certain ways.

But now (section 154) he notices a difficulty that was somewhat later pointed out to Russell by the mathematician M. H. A. Newman in a review article. If a statement to the effect that there are relations having certain properties and are instantiated in certain ways is framed entirely in logico-mathematical terms then it can be satisfied in any set of sufficient size. For the relations in question can be taken to be suitably chosen sets of ordered pairs, triples, and the like, and the suitable choice is possible provided enough elements are available. (I shall exhibit a more detailed version of this argument when we inspect the related argument by Putnam below.)

Thus Carnap writes in section 154, about the argument that he had given to support his claim that the elimination is possible, that he had assumed that:

> [...] after a replacement of one set of basic relations by another, the constructional formulas of the system would not remain applicable [...]. However, our assumption is justified only if the new relation extensions are not arbitrary, unconnected pair lists, but if we require of them that they correspond to some experienceable, "natural" relations (to give a preliminary, vague expression).

If no such requirement is made, then there are certainly other relation extensions for which all constructional formulas can be produced.

In other words, he admits that if the 'suitable choice' of sets of ordered pairs is unconstrained, if they can be 'unconnected pair lists', then a theory so framed will be true provided only there are enough elements to choose the

15 Carnap (1967), section 153.

pairs from. Practically all empirical content would be lost, in such a structuralist reconstruction of a scientific theory!

> In contrast to relations of this sort [unconnected lists of pairs], we wish to call relation extensions which correspond to experienceable, "natural" relations *founded relation extensions.*[16]

So one of the properties to be attributed to relations is this 'foundedness'. A scientific theory will be reconstructed as an assertion to the effect that there are *founded* relations instantiated in a certain pattern.

But does this not give up entirely on the structuralist program he had announced? That a relation is 'experienceable', 'natural' is not something that can be formulated using only logical vocabulary. Carnap sees this very well, and makes what seems in retrospect a desperate move. He submits, though guardedly, that this "founded" is itself a new logical term: "It is perhaps permissible, because of this generality, to envisage *foundedness* as a basic concept of logic." But this concept was introduced in an analysis of how one might add non-logical content or reference to a structure description!

Russell originally reacted to the problem of the structure of physical space by insisting that we have knowledge that goes beyond what can be mathematically represented. He insisted at that point that we are acquainted with the physical congruence relation, whose mathematical representation is just one of many congruence relations that can be imposed on a projective space. One of the latter has a privileged epistemic status, it is the one that 'enters' our experience.

Now we see Carnap opting for a precisely similar solution to the problem as it appears before him. He assigns a privileged epistemic status to certain relations, and connects that status with what can be experienced.

The history of this problem has further intermediate chapters, involving especially Reichenbach; but the problem re-emerged most strikingly some four decades later with a lecture by Reichenbach's student Hilary Putnam.

16 Carnap (1967), ibid.

3 PUTNAM'S PARADOX

At the American Philosophical Association in 1976, Putnam produced his most famous argument against metaphysical realism. He called it his model-theoretic argument. David Lewis called it Putnam's Paradox, because, he claimed, this argument would show that almost any theory at all is true. For Lewis, therefore, the argument can be cited in support of a stronger realism than the realism that Putnam targeted, a stronger realism which can resist the argument. I will begin with what I shall call the core of the argument.[17]

3.1 The argument

Suppositions

(1) THE WORLD has infinitely many pieces.
(2) Theory T is consistent.
(3) Theory T says that there are infinitely many things.

17 I'll quote here the argument as it was originally presented to the APA in 1976 (in which that core is not isolated): "So let T1 be an ideal theory, by our lights. Lifting restrictions to our actual all-too-finite powers, we can imagine T1 to have every property except objective truth – which is left open – that we like. E. g. T1 can be imagined complete, consistent, to predict correctly all observation sentences (as far as we can tell), to meet whatever 'operational constraints' there are [...], to be 'beautiful', 'simple', 'plausible', etc. [...].
I imagine that THE WORLD has (or can be broken into) infinitely many pieces. I also assume T1 says there are infinitely many things (so in this respect T1 is 'objectively right' about THE WORLD). Now T1 is consistent [...] and has (only) infinite models. So by the completeness theorem [...], T1 has a model of every infinite cardinality. Pick a model M of the same cardinality as THE WORLD. Map the individuals of M one-to-one into the pieces of THE WORLD, and use the mapping to define relations of M directly in THE WORLD. The result is a satisfaction relation SAT – a 'correspondence' between the terms of [the language] L and sets of pieces of THE WORLD – such that theory T1 comes out true – true of THE WORLD – provided we just interpret 'true' as TRUE(SAT). So whatever becomes of the claim that even the ideal theory T1 might really be false?" (Putnam (1978), pp. 125-126)

Exactly one meta-mathematical result will be required in the proof; after that it will proceed precisely like Newman's argument against Russell. That result is the Loewenheim-Skolem-Tarski-Vaught theorem, which shows that if a theory has an infinite model then it has models of every infinite cardinality.[18]

Argument

(1) Since T is consistent and has (only) infinite models, it has a model of the same cardinality as THE WORLD. (This follows from the theorem.)

(2) Let Φ be a one-to-one correspondence between the elements of that model and the pieces of the world. (This correspondence exists by definition, given that the two sets have the same cardinality.)

(3) Each term of the theory will have an extension in the model;
DO: assign to each term precisely the image under Φ of its extension in the model. Take that image to be its extension in THE WORLD.

(4) Since all the theorems of T are true in the model (i.e. given the terms' extensions in the model) all of them will also be true in THE WORLD when given those images as extensions in THE WORLD.

(5) So T is a true theory about THE WORLD.

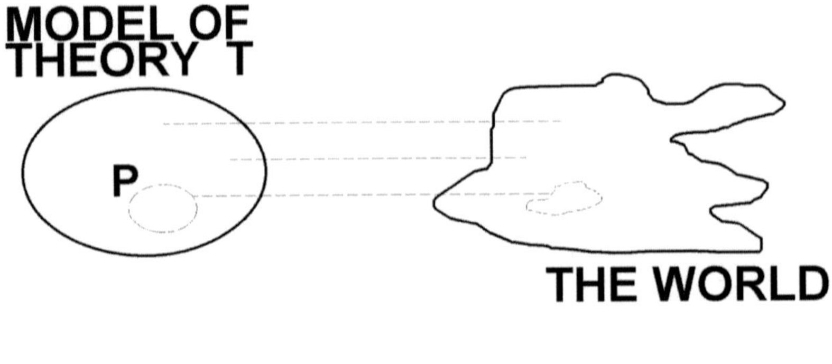

18 This theorem was initially debated in the context of philosophy of mathematics, in connection with Skolem's relativism. One spoke there also of the Loewenheim-Skolem paradox.

3.2 An example, an objection, and a realist 'way out' (?)

Let's think about an example of a simple theory and see how Putnam's argument applies.

A1) There are infinitely many distinct bodies of water.
A2) There are infinitely many things that are not water.

Assume that THE WORLD is or can be regarded as having infinitely many things in it. Then there is an extension that can be assigned to the phrase "body of water" such that both A1 and A2 come out true.

That is not very surprising! But Putnam suggests that we add an extra axiom for every assertion we want to make – or if you like, every one that is ever in the fullness of time observed to be true – of the form "X is a body of water" or "Y is not a body of water". Then there will still exist an assignment of referents to the terms 'X', 'Y' and the like, and an extension to "body of water" which will make A1, A2, and all the extra axioms true. And so forth: for the argument is very general, and does not rely on any specific assumptions about the content of the theory.

Whatever constraints we want to introduce Putnam challenges us to make explicit; then he will add them to the theory under consideration … all those constraints are after all 'just more theory'.

David Lewis then offered the following way out. When Putnam writes "Map the individuals of M one-to-one into the pieces of THE WORLD, and use the mapping to define relations of M directly in THE WORLD" Lewis insists that we must add "in such a way that the defined relations in THE WORLD are *natural* relations". The distinction between natural and unnatural relations does not enter into the formulation of the theory, it refers to a *distinction in nature* which must be observed. Must be observed how? We can understand the theory as a non-trivial assertion about what things are like only on an interpretation of the terms as referring to natural relations.

The terminological link with the passage I quoted from Carnap about 'foundedness' is not accidental: we have here essentially the same solution to essentially the same problem faced by the offered conception of science.

What is this postulated distinction in nature? Plato is said to have touched on it with his famous phrase "carving nature at the joints". Since the distinction would have no bite if it were 'just more theory' (as it would be if we simply added it to the theory), it is something not imagined to be explained or described in science. One sometimes hears an item of faith: that the relations that will ultimately be described in successful science are precisely the natural ones. But of course what cannot be meant here is "described in structural terms" – unless one were to count "natural" as structural, more or less as Carnap wanted to count "founded" as logical, and with no better reason.

4 DOING WITHOUT METAPHYSICS

I began with the assertion that science represents the phenomena by means of mathematical models. We have seen two problems for this concept of science. As Weyl points out, mathematical representation does not cut across isomorphism. As a result, distinct parts of nature may be represented in precisely the same way – so if such a representation is all that science gives us, then it does not give us differentiating knowledge of those parts. Thus it seems that to have specific knowledge of one of such a pair, we must know more than that it is adequately represented by science – but what could this extra-scientific knowledge be?

What we have seen so far are mainly metaphysical solutions. Russell, Carnap, and Lewis all postulate distinctions in nature that give a privileged status in nature to certain sets and relations. A scientific theory is then conceived of as the assertion that a certain family of relations with this privileged status has a certain structure, which is adequately represented by some mathematical model offered by the theory for that role. For example, in Russell's case, what physics says about physical space is said to be that the *real* physical congruence relation singles out Euclidean space, or alternatively a certain non-Euclidean space. On this construal, although a scientific theory, despite having only mathematical resources for representation, still has non-vacuous empirical content, unlike the corresponding pure mathematics that it uses.

To postulate such distinctions in nature is to bring in a metaphysical supplement to science. There are many objections, questions, and difficulties of detail that we could bring forward here. But instead I want to address the main question directly: Can we have a conception of science according to which its resources for representation do not extend beyond what can be done with mathematical models, but which does not fall prey to the two problems we have seen, and yet does without such metaphysics?

4.1 Asserting a relation between phenomena and model

To say that certain phenomena are accommodated in some model, we must be able to describe both the phenomena and the models. Suppose first that the former is done by means of a scientific representation (perhaps in an older or more rudimentary form) then we face the question raised by Weyl and by Carnap. We should be able to say whether we are talking of persons or villages (to quote Carnap), but the structure of the representation may be the same in both cases. In that case the scientific description does not single out either one. Suppose then that needs be we identify the phenomena in some other way, not by means of a scientific representation: do we need for this some epistemic access that is ultra-scientific, even ultra-empirical?

It is tempting to just rest in common sense here: obviously we do refer to phenomena and describe them and then assess whether a given sort of model can accommodate them. But is the former something which cannot be done by means of a scientific description? We have to face Weyl's point. When two objects are represented by isomorphic structures – hence, when their representation presents no difference between them – we may still know that they are *distinct* and in un-represented ways *different* objects. Must we embrace one of the following alternatives, apparently forced on us – namely, that

- either the point about isomorphism and mathematics is mistaken, or
- scientific representation is not at bottom mathematical representation alone, or
- science is necessarily incomplete in a way we can know it to be, or
- those apparent differences to us are illusory?

4.2 *Cutting through isomorphism: the Essential Indexical*

A map is a model. It is a model of a city, a country, a continent, or of a railway system or subway, or campus shuttle route. In each case it is very selective, as is all representation – and we can describe separately the aspects of its domain that are represented. But there is a more crucial point: a map is of no use to the traveller unless s/he can indicate some point and some orientation so as to say "I am here, facing in this direction".

Does it follow from this that a map which lacks a "you are here" tag is incomplete? Certainly not: in fact if it has such a tag, it is not transportable as maps are meant to be – in fact, what the mapmaker has done here is to take a map and make it the main ingredient of a signpost, which is not the same as a map, and is not (though it incorporates) a map.

This point about maps generalizes to a point about models in general. It is not a new point: it was crucial to Kant's 'Copernican' revolution in philosophy. Kant made this point in several ways, somewhere between his conviction that absolute space and time are forced upon us and his transcendental turn:

> No matter how well I may know the order of the compass points, I can only determine directions by reference to them, if I am aware of whether this order runs from right to left or from left to right, and the most precise map of the heavens [...] would not enable me [without this orientation] to infer [...] on which side of the horizon I ought to look for the sunrise.[19]

19 Kant (1992), p. 367. The full text is this: "Wenn ich auch noch so gut die Ordnung der Abteilungen des Horizonts weiss, so kann ich doch die Gegenden darnach nur bestimmen, indem ich mir bewusst bin, nach welcher Hand diese Ordnung fortlaufe, und die allergenaueste Himmelskarte, wenn ausser der Lage der Sterne untereinander nicht noch durch die Stellung des Abrisses gegen meine Hände die Gegend determiniert würde, so genau wie ich sie auch in Gedanken hätte, würde mich doch nicht in den Stand setzen, aus einer bekannten Gegend, z. E. Norden, zu wissen, auf welcher Seite des Horizonts ich den Sonnenaufgang zu suchen hätte."; Kant (1983), pp. 995f.

There is here a *precise and perfect analogy between theory, model, and map.* The point about the map, made already by Kant, applies to a model of any sort, and thence – within the model theoretic viewpoint that Putnam exploits – to a theory formulated in sentences as well.

4.3 Return to our epistemological question

After introducing Weyl's text and examining the four options that it appeared to offer us, I said that we face here a perplexing epistemological question:

Is there something that I could know to be the case, and which is not expressed by a proposition that could be part of some scientific theory?

The answer is YES: something expressed only by an indexical proposition. For to use a theory or model, to base predictions on it, we have to locate ourselves with respect to it. We have to be able to say, for example, that the phenomenon *we are presently witnessing* is classified in the theory as oxidizing, or as phlogiston escape, or the like. We have to locate our situation in the theory's logical space, in a way that is similar to our "We are here" with respect to a map.

But this implies no relevant incompleteness in the theory or model itself. To make this point about science is not to deny that science is (in principle?) so complete that every fact, every phenomenon, is completely represented (representable?) within science. A New York subway map or Paris Metro map is not incomplete because it comes without a "you are here" tag. It is selective, it neither does nor purports to represent more than certain aspects of the topological structure of the system – but this it does completely.

On the other hand, the extra that we need to know in order to bring a theory or model into our practice is not something that could be supplied within that theory or model. Suppose that at noon on Monday May 30, 2005 I had found a map of Münster with on it a tag "location of BvF's use of a Münster map at noon on Monday May 30, 2005". This would still have been no use to me unless I could have oriented myself with respect to it, and been able to say "I am BvF, it is now noon on …".

To paraphrase Kant: the most precise map of Muenster would not enable me, without this self-orientation, to infer on which side I ought to look for the University.

APPENDIX: RE PUTNAM

It may not be obvious how these last reflections dissolve 'Putnam's Paradox'. We should begin by noting that Putnam himself did not present the argument as a paradox, but as an argument against what he called metaphysical realism; and that he clearly signalled how the apparent paradox dissolves upon scrutiny.

We should make a sharp distinction between how his argument applies to an arbitrary language under study, and how we could apply it ourselves to our own language. An arbitrary language under study is in need of an interpretation. If we can keep the pragmatic dimension as fixed or given for the time being, that interpretation must certainly have at least as core an assignment of extensions to its singular and general terms. But focus now on the instructions in the text of his argument. They are instructions to us to do something, and include as implicature that we can do them. We are being led through a chain of reasoning destined to the conclusion that we can regard the WORLD as having a certain structure. There exists a model of the WORLD's cardinality, there exists a function that will map the one onto the other ... Select one of each! Under what conditions can we do that?

"We can regard the WORLD as having that structure." That is an assertion about us; and what is its basis? The basis is the argument that there exists a certain function which maps the model and WORLD one-to-one onto each other. Fine, that function exists – but what does that have to do with us? We have an interpretation for the given language only if we can define or identify such a function. To do that we must be able to describe both the function's domain and its range, hence both the syntax of that language and THE WORLD, as well as the way in which the former gets mapped on to the latter. Given such a description, whether the theory is true under that interpretation depends entirely on how that mapping is made. Putnam spells this out quite clearly. In "Realism and Reason", where the argument was first introduced, he defuses one point with the laconic "because the world is not describable independently of our description" (p. 496). And in "Two philosophical perspectives" he is very explicit:

> This simply states in mathematical language the intuitive fact that to single out a correspondence between two domains one needs some independent access to both domains.[20]

It is of no earthly relevance to know that there exists some such function such that it, if only it could be described, would furnish an interpretation under which the theory is true. The only question of interest for us, if we do really have such an interpretation, is whether the theory is true under *that* interpretation.

What happens now if we want to apply Putnam's argument to our own theories formulated in *our own language*? We shall be able to grasp such a theory if we can grasp an interpretation of the language in which it is formulated (i.e. our language!). Well, as noted, we can grasp an interpretation – i.e. function linking words to parts of THE WORLD – *only if we can identify and describe that function.* But we cannot do *that* unless we can independently describe THE WORLD. So Putnam's model theoretic argument, if applied to our own language, meets up with a dilemma:

(A) if we cannot describe the relevant elements of THE WORLD, neither can we describe/define/identify any function that assigns extensions to our predicates in THE WORLD;
(B) if we can describe those elements of THE WORLD then we can also distinguish between right and wrong assignments of extensions to our predicates in THE WORLD.

For example, on alternative (B), we would insist that a right assignment of an extension to "water" is water, and that all other assignments are wrong. That the theory is true on some such assignment or other is simply irrelevant to whether it is true.

20 Putnam (1981), p. 74.

It seems to me that this is also how Putnam meant it to be resolved. Note the crucial role of the indexical: just as a map says nothing to us if we cannot locate ourselves with respect to it, so a theory says nothing to us unless we can locate ourselves, in our own language, with respect to its content.

REFERENCES

Carnap, Rudolf (1967): *Der logische Aufbau der Welt.* Tr. Rolf A. George, *The Logical Structure of the World.* Berkeley: University of California Press.

Coffa, Alberto (1986): "From geometry to tolerance: sources of conventionalism in nineteenth-century geometry", in Colodny (1986), pp. 3-70.

Colodny, R. G. (1986): *From Quarks to Quasars. Philosophical Problems of Modern Physics.* Pittsburgh: University of Pittsburgh Press.

Helmholtz, Hermann von (1956): "Ueber den Ursprung und die Bedeutung der geometrischen Axiome". Tr. J. R. Newman, "On the origin and significance of geometrical axioms", pp. 647-668, in J. R. Newman, *The World of Mathematics*, vol. 1. New York: Simon and Schuster.

Kant, I. (1992): "Concerning the ultimate ground of the differentiation of directions in space", pp. 361-372, in David Walford, tr. ed., *Immanuel Kant: Theoretical Philosophy, 1755-1770.* Cambridge: Cambridge University Press.

Kant, I. (1983): "Von dem ersten Grunde des Unterschiedes der Gegenden im Raume", pp. 991-1000, in I. Kant, *Werke in Zehn Bänden*, (herausgegeben von W. Weischedel), Band 2: *Vorkritische Schriften bis 1768, Zweiter Teil.* Darmstadt: Wissenschaftliche Buchgesellschaft.

Putnam, Hilary (1976): "Realism and reason", Presidential Address to the Eastern Division of the American Philosophical Association, December 1976; reprinted in Putnam (1978), pp. 123-140.

Putnam, Hilary (1978). *Meaning and the Moral Sciences.* New York: Routledge.

Putnam, Hilary (1981): *Reason, Truth and History.* Cambridge, Mass.: Cambridge University Press.

Russell, Bertrand (1912/1959): *Problems of Philosophy.* Reprinted Oxford: Oxford University Press.

Russell, Bertrand (1927): *The Analysis of Matter*, New York: Harcourt, Brace.

Torretti, Roberto (1984): *Philosophy of Geometry from Riemann to Poincaré.* Dordrecht: Reidel.

Weyl, Herman (1934): *Mind and Nature.* Philadelphia: University of Pennsylvania Press.

OBSERVABILITY AND THE EPISTEMIC COMMUNITY

Simone Bahrenberg, Andreas Berg-Hildebrand, Carolin Köhne, Gordon Leonhard, Bernd Prien

Abstract: This paper deals with an aspect of van Fraassen's notion of observability which is central for constructive empiricism. We will argue that there is a tension between van Fraassen's claims, on the one hand, that observability is an objective matter of fact and, on the other hand, that observability is a function of the epistemic community. This is because membership in the epistemic community depends on moral and ideological criteria, so that observability in the last resort depends on these criteria, which do not seem to be objective. Therefore observability is not an objective property, either.

Keywords: constructive empiricism, observability, epistemic community

INTRODUCTION

In our paper, we will be concerned with an aspect of constructive empiricism, a view Bas van Fraassen has introduced in his book *The Scientific Image*. More precisely, we will examine the observable/unobservable distinction and its connection to the concept of the epistemic community. In our view, the characterizations van Fraassen gives of the observable/unobservable distinction and the epistemic community deserve further attention. First, we will examine the function of the observable/unobservable distinction and its connection to the notion of the epistemic community in van Fraassen's concept of constructive empiricism. This will be done in sections 1 and 2. Then, in section 3, we will point to an ambiguity in the concept of observability which results from these characterizations. We will argue that in van Fraassen's account what is observable in the last resort depends on what he calls moral and ideological criteria and that therefore observability is not an objective property of the entities in the world.

1 Constructive Empiricism and the Observable/Unobservable Distinction

Van Fraassen introduces his constructive empiricism as a view about the aim of science: "*Science aims to give us theories which are empirically adequate; and acceptance of a theory involves as belief only that it is empirically adequate.*" (SI, p. 12) For constructive empiricism, the notion of empirical adequacy is crucial because it replaces the notion of truth in a realist's formulation of the aim of science, i.e., "Science aims to give us theories which are *true*". For van Fraassen, a theory is empirically adequate "exactly if what it says about the observable things and events in this world is true – exactly if it 'saves the phenomena'." (SI, p. 12) Van Fraassen stresses that observability has no logical connection to existence and non-existence. Therefore, he only requires us to be *agnostic* about unobservable entities like electrons. So, it is the observability of an entity which determines the epistemic attitude a scientist should adopt towards it.

Often, in scientific practice, one has to choose between potentially indefinitely many theories which are empirically adequate, i.e., one has to *accept* one of these theories. This involves an epistemic and a pragmatic component (cf. SI, p. 13): Roughly speaking, accepting a theory can be characterized as *believing* that the theory is empirically adequate, while *being agnostic* about the ontological status of the parts of the theory which concern unobservable entities, while still *acting* as if one believes in them. In sum, the distinction between the observable and the unobservable is essential for differentiating between constructive empiricism and scientific realism. Therefore an appropriate and clear-cut account of this distinction is crucial for the position of constructive empiricism.

In order to see whether van Fraassen can provide such a distinction, we will now take a closer look at van Fraassen's account of the notion 'observable'. As a first rough characterization, a phenomenon is observable, according to van Fraassen, if it is possible for us to observe this phenomenon in principle, at some time, by our unaided senses. "The principle is: X is observable if there are circumstances which are such that, if X is present to us under those circumstances, then we observe it." (SI, p. 16) Therefore, van Fraassen maintains that experiential information is limited to those entities and processes that are accessible by means of our unaided senses and which are therefore regarded as observable. Electrons and bacteria, on the other hand, are regarded as unobservable entities because they are only accessible by means of measuring instruments. Van Fraassen concedes that there are unclear cases, but in his opinion this does not mean that we cannot make use of the predicate 'observable' or that it doesn't apply to anything: 'Observable' may be a vague predicate, but vague predicates can still be useful, and do apply, as long as there are clear cases (of observable and unobservable entities).

The following trait of the notion of observability will be important for our purposes: Usually, 'observable' is understood as a two-place predicate expressing a relation between a thing and an individual organism: a thing X is observable for an individual organism Y. However, in the characterization of constructive empiricism, van Fraassen uses 'observable' differently: In this context, observability is not understood with reference to an individual organism, but with reference to an epistemic community of organisms. It will prove important to distinguish both uses of 'observable' mentioned here: Observable for an individual organism and observable for an epistemic community.

2 Observability and the Epistemic Community

In order to show that there is a tension within van Fraassen's theory concerning the observable/unobservable distinction, we will point out, in this section, that the property of observability in the final analysis hinges on moral and ideological criteria. As we have just said, van Fraassen understands the observable/unobservable distinction as referring to an epistemic community and not to individual organisms: "What counts as an observable phenomenon is a function of what the epistemic community is (that *observable* is *observable-to-us*)"

(SI, p. 19).[1] So it is the epistemic community that draws the line between observable and unobservable phenomena (for an epistemic community).

We think that the reason why van Fraassen understands observable as referring to the epistemic community is that epistemic attitudes (i.e., belief vs. acceptance) cannot be allowed to vary within an epistemic community. Scientific inquiry could not be carried out as a common enterprise if some scientists believed claims that others only accepted. Since the appropriate epistemic attitudes, however, depend on the observability of phenomena, this could happen if observability were understood with reference to individual organisms because the observational abilities of the different organisms might differ.

The next point to note is that van Fraassen thinks that a change of the epistemic community is possible:

> Significant encounters with dolphins, extraterrestrials, or the products of our own genetic engineering may lead us to widen the epistemic community. And this community could in any case have been different from what it was. I feel no great difficulty with thought experiments about such eventualities. (EPS, p. 256)

Whether or not we accept someone as a member of our epistemic community depends, according to van Fraassen, on moral and ideological considerations:

> At present, we count the human race as the epistemic community to which we belong; but this race may mutate, or that community may be increased by adding other animals (terrestrial or extra-terrestrial) through relevant ideological or moral decisions ('to count them as persons'). (SI, p. 18)

That this is van Fraassen's position is also made clear by his reaction to a thought experiment proposed by Paul Churchland. In this thought experiment Churchland imagines that we encounter humanoids who each of them

1 See also: "to accept a theory is (for us) to believe that it is empirically adequate – that what the theory says *about what is observable* (by us) is true." (SI, p. 18)

have an electron microscope permanently in place before their left eye. Because of this they are able to observe things like DNA strands or bacteria.[2] In his reply to Churchland, van Fraassen says that it is possible that we "have accepted these humanoids as persons, as members of our epistemic community". (EPS, p. 256) In this quote, van Fraassen speaks of the acceptance of persons. Since he has also used this expression in the previous quote from *The Scientific Image*, it seems clear that the moral and ideological criteria mentioned above are involved here as well.

Unfortunately, van Fraassen nowhere tells us what exactly the moral and ideological criteria are that decide whether or not we should accept an organism as a person. So, we would like to hear more about what these criteria are, and about what the process of acceptance of an organism as a person looks like. Do organisms have to meet certain physical requirements to be eligible as persons? Could we, for example, accept a single humanoid with an electron microscope or could we only incorporate a whole community of humanoids into ours? Van Fraassen should say more about these and other questions.[3]

We would like to make one suggestion as to what these moral and ideological criteria might look like. There seems to be the following constraint on the criteria of membership in the epistemic community: It is an important trait of the epistemic community that we rely on the testimony of others. Science as a common enterprise does not seem to be possible if scientists could not rely on each other's claims.[4] Correspondingly, the moral and ideological criteria should be such as to admit only organisms that are in some sense epistemically trustworthy. I.e., the claims of these organisms should have at least some degree of reliability. Of course, making this suggestion is still a long way from specifying criteria of membership.

2 Cf. Churchland (1985), pp. 43-44.

3 In discussion, van Fraassen has conceded that the concept of a person has to be clarified, though he claimed that this is not a task for the philosophy of science. In any case, we wonder whether this clarification can be given without getting involved with the kind of metaphysics van Fraassen rejects.

4 Cf. Seager (1988), p. 184.

3 Observability and Objectivity

So, we would like to urge van Fraassen to say more about the process of the extension of the epistemic community and the relevant criteria. The main thrust of this paper, however, is to show that there is a tension between van Fraassen's claim that observability is an objective property and his views about membership in the epistemic community. The next step on the way to doing this is noting that according to van Fraassen, a change in the epistemic community leads to a change of what is observable:

> [S]uppose that we have accepted these humanoids as persons, as members of our epistemic community. In that case we have already broadened the extension of *us*, and what is observable to them is observable. (EPS, p. 256)

So, which phenomena are observable and which are not depends on who is a member of our epistemic community. If we broaden the extension of the epistemic community to organisms which can observe with their unaided senses phenomena which we (the current members of the epistemic community) cannot observe, we can say "what is observable to them is observable" (EPS, p. 256), i.e., observable to the extended epistemic community. So, by extending the epistemic community we can sometimes extend the range of observable phenomena. Consequently, whether we can believe a certain proposition or must confine ourselves to accepting it also depends on who is a member of the epistemic community.

We have seen that the observability of a phenomenon depends on who is a member of the epistemic community and we have seen that membership in the epistemic community depends on moral and ideological criteria. Consequently, whether or not a phenomenon is observable in the last analysis depends on moral and ideological criteria. We have noted that van Fraassen does not tell us anything about what these criteria are. But whatever these criteria are, it seems doubtful that they are objective in the sense in which findings of the natural sciences are objective. Because of this lack of objectivity, there even seems to be a threat of arbitrariness concerning our decisions to extend the epistemic community.

For this reason it also seems doubtful whether observability is an objective matter of fact. Whether or not we should, for example, accept the electron-microscope-humanoids as members of our epistemic community is determined by moral criteria that do not seem to be objective. Consequently, the observability of bacteria which these humanoids can observe is not an objective matter of fact, either.

However, in many places it seems as if van Fraassen regards the property of observability as completely objective. Consider for example the following quote:

> What can be observed, and what there really is to be observed, is a matter of fact – it is not theory-, mind-, or language-dependent, but is there regardless of whether we even so much as pay attention to it. (LE, p. 55)

Van Fraassen stresses here the independence of observability of our theories, minds, and language. We take this to mean that observability is also independent of moral and ideological criteria which can hardly be regarded as objective.

In *The Scientific Image* van Fraassen states that "the human organism is, from the point of view of physics, a certain kind of measuring apparatus." (SI, p. 17) And he argues that the observability of a phenomenon is a question that is settled by the final physics and biology and that this question therefore is an objective matter:

> As such [the sensory apparatus] has certain inherent limitations – which will be described in detail in the final physics and biology. It is these limitations to which the 'able' in 'observable' refers – our limitations *qua* human beings. (SI, p. 17)

The reference to the final physics and biology seems to us to indicate that van Fraassen would like to regard observability as an objective property.

We agree that the final physics will determine objectively whether or not a phenomenon is observable for an individual organism or for a kind of organism. (In order to determine observability for humans, for example, one could use the idea of an ideal exemplar of the natural kind 'human being'. What is observable to such an organism is observable to humans.) However, this objective determination always presupposes that certain subjects of observation (i.e., certain organisms that observe) are given. Thus the final physics can only determine observability for an epistemic community if it is already clear which organisms, or kinds of organism, belong to the epistemic community. So, an appeal to the final physics is of no help with regard to the problem we are raising here: Namely that the criteria for membership in the epistemic community do not seem to be objective and that therefore the property of being observable does not seem to be objective, either.

Conclusion

Our examination of van Fraassen's notion of observability has led to the somewhat surprising result that observability in the last resort depends on moral and ideological criteria. Therefore, it is *prima facie* implausible that observability is an objective fact. So, the epistemic attitudes one should undertake according to constructive empiricism depend on moral and ideological decisions. This is quite surprising because there seems to be a certain arbitrariness in such decisions, especially when it is largely unclear on what basis these decisions rest.

If van Fraassen wants to insist on the objectivity of observability, he should not define this notion in terms of the epistemic community. To put it the other way round, if he wants to retain the connection between observability and the epistemic community, he owes us an explanation of how the moral decisions concerning membership in the epistemic community rest on objective facts.

REFERENCES

Churchland, Paul (1985): "The Ontological Status of Observables: In Praise of the Super-empirical Virtues", Churchland & Hooker (1985), pp. 25-47.

Churchland, Paul & Clifford Hooker (eds.) (1985): *Images of Science. Essays on Realism and Empiricism, with a Reply from Bas C. van Fraassen.* Chicago: University of Chicago Press 1985.

Seager, William (1988): "Scientific Anti-realism and the Epistemic Community", *PSA* 1988, vol. 1, pp. 181-187.

TO BE PRUSSIAN OR NOT TO BE PRUSSIAN

Van Fraassen and the Inference to the Best Explanation

Jochen Apel, Nikola Kompa, Sebastian Schmoranzer, Jörg Steinhaus

Abstract: Scientific realists commonly argue for the existence of unobservable entities by means of an inference to the best explanation. In contrast to that van Fraassen holds that knowledge about the existence of such entities is beyond our ken. Therefore he develops three arguments against abductive reasoning. We try to show that i) the argument from the bad lot is either under-defended or leads to radical scepticism, ii) the argument from indifference is either useless or needs further support, iii) the Dutch Book argument – as it stands – seems to prove too much.

Keywords: scientific realism, inference to the best explanation, abductive reasoning, argument from the bad lot, argument from indifference, Dutch-Book argument

> The difference is analogous to that between (or so Justice Oliver Wendell Holmes wrote) the Prussian and the English concept of law. In the former everything is forbidden which is not explicitly permitted, and in the latter, everything permitted that is not forbidden. (LS, p. 171)

1

Are there unobservable entities such as electrons independently of whether there are human beings thinking about the world? Van Fraassen is agnostic about this issue. According to him we do not know. In contrast, scientific realists are convinced that there are good reasons to believe in the existence of unobservable entities. And some think that electrons are good examples. Their typical argument runs as follows:

P1: The best available explanation for our observations in physics is that there are electrons.

P2: The best available explanation is likely to be true.

C: Therefore, it is likely that there are electrons.

This is a paradigm case of an inference to the best explanation. Of course, this kind of abductive reasoning does not yield certainty. But it gives good reasons to believe in the existence of electrons – or so it seems at least.

In order to defend his own agnostic and anti-realist position, van Fraassen formulates a rather radical critique on abduction. For van Fraassen no inference to the best explanation can ever yield good epistemic reasons to hold a belief. Be it as an inference in everyday life or as an inference in science, be it as an inference to the truth or to the empirical adequacy of a belief, in neither of these cases does it lead to justified belief.[1]

In *Laws and Symmetry* van Fraassen offers three arguments for this view. According to *the argument from the bad lot* the assumption that the best available explanation is likely to be true is not warranted. *The argument from indifference* is supposed to demonstrate that this assumption is even false. And the *Dutch Book argument* serves as an argument against probabilistic versions of the inference to the best explanation.

We will not try to defend the inference to the best explanation here.[2] Our aim is more modest. We concentrate on the argument from the bad lot and the argument from indifference and try to cast some doubt on them.

1 Ladyman et al. (1997), p. 311.

2 In this case we had to say something about the Dutch Book argument too.

2

In inferring to the best explanation it is assumed that the best available explanation is likely to be true. By means of the argument from the bad lot van Fraassen tries to display this assumption as unjustified. A closer look at van Fraassen's remarks reveals that there are three versions of the argument from the bad lot. Since our critique applies to all three versions we can focus on the following variant (LS, pp. 142f.):

P1: We are justified in the assumption that the best available explanation is likely to be true only if we are justified in thinking that the true explanation is likely to be found among the available ones.

P2: We are justified in thinking that the true explanation is likely to be found among the available ones only if we can rule out the error possibility that all available explanations are false.

P3: We cannot rule out the error possibility that all available explanations are false.

C: We are not justified in the assumption that the best available explanation is likely to be true.[3]

Stathis Psillos argues against the third premise. Given our background theories we do have good reasons for the assumption that the true explanation is among the available ones — or so he says. Psillos, however, faces a serious

3 The other versions differ in respect to the error possibility that has to be ruled out. All in all the following three error possibilities can be read out of van Fraassen's text:

EP1: All available explanations are false. (This possibility is not explicitly mentioned by van Fraassen. None the less it is central to his discussion in LS, pp. 143-145.)

EP2: All available explanations are bad explanations. ("So our selection may well be the best of a bad lot."; LS, p. 143.)

EP3: There is a better explanation than the best available one. ("So to believe the best explanation requires more than an evaluation of the given hypothesis. It requires a step beyond the comparative judgement that this hypothesis is better than its actual rivals."; LS, p. 143.)

problem. Since our background theories are themselves based on abductive reasoning he begs the question.[4]

Take the background theory of Darwinism for example. One might argue that it is likely that we are for the most part hitting the truth because otherwise we would not have survived. But Darwinism is itself based on the assumption that it best explains the development of species. Therefore, it cannot itself be used to defend the inference to the best explanation.

That all available explanations are false might be ruled out by means of enumerative induction. Often our explanations turned out to be true. Therefore, it is now likely that not all available explanations are false. Unfortunately, this argument will not do, for van Fraassen disputes all kinds of inductive inferences (LS, pp. 132, 151). Under such circumstances it is better to eschew the discussion about van Fraassen's third premise and turn to the second one. It says:

> P2: We are justified in thinking that the true explanation is likely to be found among the available ones only if we can rule out the error possibility that all available explanations are false.

Now, which principle of exclusion is the premise based on? In contemporary epistemology it is common to distinguish between a strong and a moderate principle of exclusion.

> Strong principle of exclusion: To be justified one has to rule out *every* error possibility.
>
> Moderate principle of exclusion: To be justified one has to rule out every *relevant* error possibility.

To facilitate further discussions let us call the error possibility that all explanations might be false "van Fraassen's error possibility". Now, let us suppose that van Fraassen subscribes to the moderate principle of exclusion. This would be in line with his anti-Prussian attitude that everything is permitted that is not forbidden (cf. LS, p. 171). But in that case the relevance of van

4 This Psillos readily concedes; Psillos (1996), p. 40.

Fraassen's error possibility still has to be shown – a job van Fraassen has not undertaken yet.

And this task is not to be underestimated. We have to keep in mind that van Fraassen wants to discredit *all* cases in which we apply an inference to the best explanation. Now, let us suppose that an error possibility is relevant exactly if we have reasons to think that the possibility is the situation that actually obtains. Then van Fraassen has to answer the following question: Is it true that for *every* situation in which one chooses among available explanations there are reasons to believe that *all* of them are false?

Van Fraassen could try to answer the question by pointing to the fact that *sometimes* all of our explanations turn out to be false. That is true. But van Fraassen has to offer further reasons, as the following remarks will reveal: Firstly, the fact that sometimes all explanations turn out to be false does not provide us with a reason to think that in *every* situation all explanations one considers are false. Similarly, the fact that my sense experiences sometimes lead to wrong judgments is no reason to distrust my senses in all cases. Secondly, at least in everyday life the best available explanation often turns out to be true.[5]

We do not want to say that there is no way to argue for the relevance of van Fraassen's error possibility. But this job needs to be done and it does not seem to be an easy one.

What if van Fraassen adopted a Prussian attitude and subscribed to the strong principle of exclusion instead? Then every error possibility would have to be ruled out – including van Fraassen's error possibility.

However, van Fraassen now faces two other problems: Firstly, the strong principle of exclusion is itself doubtful. In everyday life we ascribe knowledge to each other although we are not able to exclude *every* error possibility. I know that my cat has not stolen the beer cans out of my fridge even though I cannot rule out that my cat temporarily mutated into a creature with extraordinary capacities and lust for beer.

5 Besides, if van Fraassen wanted to motivate his error possibility by alluding to past failure he would have to accept some kind of inductive reasoning. Maybe van Fraassen would like to motivate his claim with the help of his argument from indifference. As we will show later, this argument is itself doubtful.

Secondly, if one accepts the strong principle of exclusion radical scepticism is inevitable.[6] On the one hand, a Humean scepticism about induction is unavoidable. If one infers from a set of observed cases to an unobserved case it is always possible that the set of observed cases is not representative. This possibility cannot be excluded without begging the question. It would be necessary to determine certain characteristic features of hitherto representative sets and to infer that all sets displaying these features are representative too.

On the other hand, a Cartesian scepticism about the external world threatens. It is possible that we are all brains in a vat. But we cannot exclude this possibility by appealing to our experience. And arguments a priori against the Cartesian hypothesis are doubtful.[7]

How problematic is the threat of radical scepticism for van Fraassen? He seems to be willing to accept a kind of Humean scepticism about induction (LS, pp. 132, 151). We should be aware of what that means: Someone who thinks that the sun will rise tomorrow is epistemically as justified in her belief as someone who thinks that the sun will never rise again.[8] Be that as it may, Cartesian scepticism is unacceptable even for van Fraassen:

> Scepticism is an ugly threat; a philosophical position which leads to scepticism reduces itself to absurdity.[9]

6 Cf. Psillos (1996), p. 37.

7 Probably, because of his empiricist attitude arguments a priori are not to van Fraassen's liking anyway. (cf. ES, pp. 42f.)

8 Could Bayesianism be a solution here? Within a Bayesian epistemology one ascribes subjective probabilities to one's beliefs. This ascription is based on prior probabilities that are modified in the light of new experience with the help of certain principles such as the Bayesian principle of conditionalization. The belief that the sun will rise tomorrow has a higher subjective probability than the belief that the sun will never rise again.
But are our subjective probabilities epistemic reasons to hold a belief? If one accepts the strong principle of exclusion we face the following problem: One would have to rule out the possibility that we were completely on the wrong track when we ascribed our prior probabilities. And one would have to exclude the possibility that our experience leading to the modification of our prior probabilities did not lead us astray. But without appeal to some kind of inductive or Bayesian reasoning such an exclusion appears to be impossible.

9 Ladyman et al. (1997), p. 317.

With respect to the argument from the bad lot the following summary can be given: Either the premise that one has to exclude the error possibility that all available explanations are false is under-defended or the premise is based on a doubtful principle of exclusion which leads to an unacceptable scepticism.[10] So let us turn our backs on the argument from the bad lot and consider the argument from indifference.

10 This conclusion also holds for the other variants of the argument from the bad lot:

Alternative version 1:

P1*: We are justified in the assumption that the best available explanation is likely to be true only if we are justified in thinking that the true explanation is likely to be found among the available explanations.

P2*: We are justified in thinking that the true explanation is likely to be found among the available explanations only if we can rule out the error possibility that all available explanations are bad explanations.

P3*: We cannot rule out the error possibility that all available explanations are bad explanations.

C*: We are not justified in the assumption that the best available explanation is likely to be true.

What about P2*? If van Fraassen accepts the moderate principle of exclusion he still has to show that in every situation there are reasons to belief that all available explanations are bad explanations. If van Fraassen accepts the strong principle of exclusion scepticism threatens.

Alternative version 2:

P1**: We are justified in the assumption that the best available explanation is likely to be true only if we are justified in thinking that the true explanation is likely to be found among the available explanations.

P2**: We are justified in thinking that the true explanation is likely to be found among the available explanations only if we can rule out the error possibility that the best explanation is not among the available explanations.

P3**: We cannot rule out the error possibility that the best explanation is not among the available explanations.

C**: We are not justified in the assumption that the best available explanation is likely to be true.

What has been said about P2* holds for P2** too.

3

The second premise in the realist inference to the best explanation says that it is likely that the best available explanation is true. Van Fraassen's argument from indifference is meant to prove this assumption false. In his eyes it is even likely that the best available explanation is false. In *Laws and Symmetry* he argues as follows (LS, p. 146):

> P1: Beside the best available explanation there are many (or even infinitely many) equally good but unborn explanations which are incompatible with the best available one.
>
> P2: Any one of these explanations is as likely to be true as any other.
>
> C: It is not very likely that the best available explanation is true.[11]

As Psillos rightly remarks, van Fraassen does not offer a reason for the first premise although it is anything but evidently true.[12] In a reply to Psillos van Fraassen asserts the following:

> for the argument from indifference to go through, it is irrelevant whether T *possibly* is a random member of a class of equally good explanations or whether T *actually* is a member of such a class; [...].[13]

Well, this is certainly not the case. The proposed modification of the first premise of van Fraassen's argument leads to a totally different conclusion. His argument then runs as follows:

> P1': *It is possible that* there are many (or even infinitely many) unborn explanations beside the best available explanation which are equally good and incompatible with it.
>
> P2': Any one of these explanations is as likely to be true as any other.
>
> C': *It is possible that* it is not very likely that the best available explanation is true.

11 One might wonder what conception of probability is in play here and whether it is the same in premise P2 and the conclusion.

12 Psillos (1996), p. 43.

13 Ladyman et al. (1997), p. 309.

This conclusion sounds rather strange. What exactly does it mean that it is possible that something is very likely?[14] But even taken cum grano salis the conclusion does not serve van Fraassen's purpose anymore. He wants to refute the assumption that it *is* very likely that the best available explanation is true. But that the best explanation is likely to be true is compatible with the claim that it is *possibly* very *unlikely* that it is true.

Maybe there is another way out. In an anti-Prussian spirit van Fraassen could stick to the original version of his argument and defend the first premise as follows: Every claim is innocent until proved guilty. Therefore the assumption that there are always many equally good unborn rivals to the best available explanation does not stand in need of justification anymore.

But this reasoning will not do. First of all, we could make a similar move for the denial of van Fraassen's premise. One could say: Unless there are reasons to the contrary it is justified to assume that there are *not* many good unborn explanations. We are caught in a deadlock. The question now is: Whose assumption is better off?

Van Fraassen tries to motivate his premise that there are always many equally good unborn explanations as follows:

> [H]owever, we know that we are not dealing with a mere possibility here. Fundamental physics provides us with some well known examples of empirically equivalent theories. (Recently much in the limelight: Bohm's mechanics, which is demonstrably empirically equivalent to elementary quantum mechanics.)[15]

What does this remark prove? Van Fraassen has shown that sometimes there are empirically equivalent theories. He has not shown that there are always many equally good explanations.

Let it be granted that we can always construct infinitely many explanations which are empirically equivalent to the best available one. Still, by van Fraassen's own theory there is more to an explanation than empirical ade-

14 To answer this question one would have to say more about the concepts of possibility and probability involved in the conclusion.

15 Ladyman et al. (1997), p. 310.

quacy. The fact that two theories are empirically equivalent does not mean that they have the same explanatory value (cf. SI, pp. 97, 100).

According to van Fraassen's own account of explanation, explanations are answers to why-questions. And the value of an answer partially depends on whether it is an answer to questions that are of interest to us. Therefore, whether an explanation is a good one is a highly interest-relative matter. And this makes it even more unlikely that there is always a number of explanations which stand on a par as far as empirical adequacy and epistemic interests are concerned (cf. SI, pp. 98-156).

Regarding the argument from indifference we can therefore conclude: Due to the interest-relativity of explanations van Fraassen's claim that there are always many (or even infinitely many) unborn explanations which are as good as the best available explanation is rather doubtful. And van Fraassen's modified version of the argument from indifference is useless.

4

Let us take stock: Inferences to the best explanation serve as arguments in favor of scientific realism. Since van Fraassen defends some kind of anti-realist position within the philosophy of science he has to find some arguments against such inferences. Van Fraassen's critique of abductive reasoning is rather radical. Such reasoning never leads to justified belief. We have examined two arguments van Fraassen adduces in support of his view: the argument from the bad lot and the argument from indifference. Both arguments are problematic. The argument from the bad lot depends on the premise that one always has to rule out that all available explanations are false in order for the inference to the best explanation to go through. But this assumption is either under-defended or it depends on a strong principle of exclusion which is itself doubtful and leads to radical scepticism.

The argument from indifference also depends on a premise which stands, to say the least, in need of further support. It is rather doubtful, that there are always many unborn explanations which are as good as the best explanation available. And the modified version of the argument from indifference was shown to be useless.

We have to be fair, however. We did not discuss van Fraassen's Dutch Book argument which is both ingenious and intricate. Surely, it is worth an article of its own.[16] Even though we cannot discuss it here, we would like to finish with a brief remark concerning some consequences of the Dutch Book argument.

The upshot of the argument is as follows: Every person who modifies the subjective probabilities of her beliefs by according bonus probabilities to the best explanation available becomes incoherent in the following way: She will be willing to accept a set of wagers such that under all circumstances she will loose. In short, she will fall victim to a Dutch Book. But now van Fraassen says something strange:

> Someone who comes to hold a belief because he found it explanatory is not thereby irrational. He becomes irrational, however, if he adopts it as a rule to do so, and even more if he regards us as rationally compelled by it. (LS, p. 142)

So one might rationally accept a given hypothesis because one finds it explanatory. One becomes irrational only if one adopts the inference to the best explanation as a rule. And one becomes irrational because one becomes vulnerable to Dutch Books.

But then it seems as if the Dutch Book Argument proves too much. For what difference does it make whether I consciously follow an inference to the best explanation or whether I just happen to reason according to it? I am vulnerable to Dutch Books either way, or so it seems.[17] So the point is that if I am subject to incoherent beliefs whenever I give a hypothesis extra credit for being explanatory, then this will be the case whether I thereby explicitly follow a rule or whether I just happen to comply with it. If the one leads to incoherent beliefs, then so does the other.

16 For a good illustration and discussion of van Fraassen's Dutch Book argument see Klärner (2003), chap. 5.

17 And the point generalizes, for van Fraassen has it that "[t]he rule of IBE, and indeed the whole species of ampliative rules, is incoherent" (LS, p. 151).

The problem is that van Fraassen wants to subscribe, in a way, to Bayesianism and also to epistemic Voluntarism. Following Jonathan Kvanvig, but simplifying a lot, the two positions can be put thus: *Bayesianism* is the claim that there is no ampliative rule of belief-revision. If one follows a rule in belief-revision, it must be a Bayesian rule, such as conditionalization. *Voluntarism*, on the other hand, is the claim that one does not need to follow a rule in order to be rational.[18] It allows for forms of reasoning that are rational although they go beyond the available evidence. So on the one hand, van Fraassen holds that any epistemic *rule* has to be non-ampliative. On the other hand, he is anxious to "give room to practices of ampliation beyond the evidence" (LS, p. 151).

But given the above consideration, it seems as if van Fraassen cannot regard the inference to the best explanation as a rational form of reasoning and at the same time hold on to the Dutch Book argument. Something has to go. Either you are or you are not a Prussian.

REFERENCES

Klärner, Holger (2003): *Der Schluß auf die beste Erklärung.* Berlin/New York: Walter de Gruyter.

Kvanvig, Jonathan, L. (1994): "A Critique of van Fraassen's Voluntaristic Epistemology", *Synthese* 98, pp. 325-348.

Ladyman, James et al. (1997): "A Defence of Van Fraassen's Critique of Abductive Inference: Reply to Psillos", *The Philosophical Quarterly* 47 (188), pp. 305-321.

Psillos, Stathis (1996): "On Van Fraassen's Critique of Abductive Reasoning", *The Philosophical Quarterly* 46 (182), pp. 31-47.

18 Cf. Kvanvig (1994), p. 325.

THE HARDSHIPS OF AN EMPIRICIST

Van Fraassen's Compromise Between Epistemic Modesty and Adequacy to Science

Andreas Berg-Hildebrand, Christian Suhm

Abstract: The paper deals with two central features of Bas van Fraassen's overall empiricist project, namely epistemic modesty and adequacy to science. After clarifying these two notions, we will try to show that there is a serious tension between the two requirements. Moreover, we interpret constructive empiricism as a compromise between them and argue that it is an unsatisfying one. Serious problems arise because van Fraassen relates epistemic modesty to the observable/unobservable distinction rather than to an observed/observable distinction. In our view, he has to reconsider either his picture of empiricism or his philosophy of science, i.e. constructive empiricism.

Keywords: constructive empiricism, epistemic modesty, adequacy to science

INTRODUCTION

Bas van Fraassen is an avowed empiricist. His philosophical work in the recent years has been mainly devoted to the questions as to what empiricism is and what it could be, if it is to be counted as a promising philosophy today. (ES, pp. 31-63) According to van Fraassen, empiricism cannot on pain of inconsistency and self-refutation be expressed by a factual thesis, such as, for instance, the claim that experience is the sole source of knowledge.[1] Rather,

1 One may wonder whether it is this bold thesis that correctly represents the core conviction of the majority of empiricists in the history of philosophy. Philosophers of various empiricist traditions may well concede that there are other sources of

empiricism is to be envisaged as a philosophical attitude or stance. (Cf. ES, pp. 40-48) The empirical stance van Fraassen recommends can, therefore, not be spelled out as a set of claims or hypotheses, but comprises a variety of attitudes, commitments, and approaches towards different topics of philosophical concern. In particular, by adopting the empirical stance one is committed to give center stage to the deliverances of experience as well as to the methods and standards of the empirical sciences.

Two aspects of van Fraassen's empiricist attitude have attracted much attention within recent philosophical debates. *First*, the empiricist – even if she does not rely on a factual thesis as regards possible sources of knowledge – commits herself to some sort of epistemic modesty, i.e. to refraining from far-reaching metaphysical speculations. *Second*, the empiricist full-heartedly admires science and its methodology. It is, therefore, of central interest to the empiricist to find an answer to the question of what science is, and to give criteria for an adequate reconstruction of science. It is these two aspects – *epistemic modesty* and *adequacy to science* – which can be regarded as essential to the overall project of van Fraassen's empiricism (cf. GRCE) and which we wish to put to scrutiny in our considerations. We will do this in section two by examining van Fraassen's position in the philosophy of science, namely constructive empiricism. Some clarifications on the notions of epistemic modesty and adequacy to science as well as on their importance for the prospects of empiricism will show that it is not at all unproblematic to stick to modesty in epistemology on the one hand, and to do justice to the demands of science on the other. As we will see, there is a strong tension between these two requirements which we will address in section three.

knowledge than experience (logical or mathematical intuition, e.g.) and thereby avoid being entangled in inconsistency and self-refutation.

1 SETTING THE STAGE

(A) *Epistemic modesty and Philosophy of Science*

Since the epistemic modesty the empiricist is committed to is fundamental to her understanding of empiricism, it is also of great importance to her conception on science. Therefore, van Fraassen is not only critical of metaphysical explanations of whatever provenance but also sets a strict limit as to what kind of belief is involved in the acceptance of a scientific theory. According to van Fraassen, "acceptance of a theory involves as belief only that it is empirically adequate" (SI, p. 12). Empirical adequacy, in turn, is stipulated as truth with regard to observable entities, i.e. as truth with regard to those parts of nature that are observable for us. (SI, pp. 12, 18; cf. also MM, pp. 482f.) Consequently, one should, as a truthful empiricist, restrict one's beliefs to observable things and remain skeptical about the existence and properties of unobservable entities to which theoretical terms in scientific theories putatively refer.[2] Although van Fraassen does not subscribe to the idea of epistemological principles, be they empiricist or other, as delivering *rational obligations* or *compelling reasons* for certain beliefs, he is clearly opting for epistemic modesty and for restricting our beliefs to observable entities. Adopting the empirical stance involves giving center stage to the deliverances of experience and refraining from beliefs the content of which reaches beyond the boundaries of observability.

If, from an empiricist point of view, it is recommended to be skeptical about the unobservable, it seems quite plausible to restrict the aim of science to providing us with theories that are empirically adequate, rather than construing scientific activity as an endeavor to discover truth *tout court*, i.e. truth with respect to observable and unobservable entities alike. In light of these considerations van Fraassen reconstructs the realism/antirealism debate in the philosophy of science as a controversy about the aim of science. And this

2 It has to be mentioned that van Fraassen's skepticism is of the agnostic sort. That means that he holds the epistemological thesis that we cannot *know* whether unobservable entities posited by scientific theories exist or not, or whether they have the properties the theories say they have.

is the core of the empiricist's philosophy of science, namely of her antirealist position van Fraassen dubbed *constructive empiricism* (CE):

> CE: *Science aims to give us theories which are empirically adequate; and acceptance of a theory involves as belief only that it is empirically adequate.* (SI, p. 12; italics by van Fraassen)

Of course, CE is not by itself an epistemological thesis, but its appeal to empirical adequacy as the central goal of scientific theorizing is strongly motivated by the empiricist's demand for epistemic modesty. As Marc Alspector-Kelly clearly pointed out, it is CE that van Fraassen sees as "congenial" to the empiricist standpoint and as being licensed by the empiricist's self-restriction to experience as a guidance for beliefs.[3] Consequently, the empiricist should also be an adherent of CE.

(B) Constructive Empiricism and Adequacy to Science

It might be objected, however, that CE provides a rather misleading portrayal of what science is after. Isn't it on closer inspection simply a fact that science as a social venture aims at providing true theories, theories that depict reality more or less correctly with respect to its observable *and* its unobservable domain? However successful science is or will be relative to its defined aim (note that both CE and the more realist claim that it is truth *tout court* that science aims at remain silent about the success of science) it seems to be much more in line with what scientists actually do and with what they claim to be the aim of their professional activity to cling to scientific realism (SR) as it is formulated by van Fraassen:

> SR: *Science aims to give us, in its theories, a literally true story of what the world is like; and acceptance of a scientific theory involves the belief that it is true.* (SI, p. 8; italics by van Fraassen)

3 Alspector-Kelly (2001), p. 417.

In light of this realist alternative, the decisive question with regard to CE seems to be the following: Can CE be conceived of as an adequate reconstruction of the aim of science? Whereas it seems plausible to endorse CE on particular *empiricist* grounds, namely the restriction of one's beliefs to observable entities, CE seems to fall short of the criterion of adequacy to scientific practice that is essential to the empiricist's admiration for science.

At this point we should – in favor of CE – take into account some qualifications with regard to van Fraassen's understanding of the expression "science aims to" and with regard to the status of CE within a comprehensive empiricist philosophy. In a response to Gideon Rosen van Fraassen stressed that, although adequacy to science and to its practice is a central criterion of any reconstruction of the aim of science, it is science *as it is viewed by an empiricist* that has to be adequately pictured in a thesis about the aim of science. (GRCE) According to van Fraassen, the aim of science is neither some abstract thing to be distilled from the individual scientists' concrete aims they pursue when doing research, nor is it something to be read off the scientific activity as such independently of what philosophical point of view one adopts. It is inevitable, so van Fraassen argues, to presuppose an understanding of what science is, in order to give an account of the aims of science that is largely independent of what scientists themselves purport to pursue when participating in scientific practices. (GRCE, pp. 188ff.) In consequence, it is no empirical (i.e. sociological) question whether CE is adequate to science. On the contrary, CE is to make good sense of what we count as scientific activity only under the presumption that we have already adopted a certain philosophical point of view. If it is the empiricist point of view – van Fraassen's empirical stance – we are committed to epistemic modesty and to adequacy to science in our reasoning about the aim of science. And our understanding of science will then be shaped by our overall empiricist admiration for science including, e.g., a positive attitude towards instrumental reliability, empirical success, correctness and precision of predictions, and so on.

(C) Balancing the Elements

With these further qualifications we are now able to evaluate the status of CE within van Fraassen's overall empiricist project. CE is the core of the empiricist's philosophy of science. According to Rosen, van Fraassen's defense of CE can be interpreted as the attempt to find a *compromise* between two commitments, namely the traditional demand of empiricists for restricting one's beliefs to the deliverances of experience on the one hand, and adequacy to science on the other.[4] Roughly, these commitments can be equated with the above mentioned ingredients of the empirical stance, namely epistemic modesty and adequacy to science.

Of course, epistemologically weaker (that means epistemically more modest) positions than CE are conceivable (e.g. manifestationalism, which is the claim that it is the aim of science to correctly describe observ*ed* instead of observ*able* entities[5]), but they would, in contrast to CE, fall short of the criterion of adequacy to science and thereby belie the empiricist's admiration for science. We shall presume for the moment that CE is the epistemologically weakest claim about the aim of science that is adequate to scientific practice. Obviously, by maintaining CE the demands for epistemic modesty and adequacy to science involved in van Fraassen's empirical stance are not fulfilled completely and to the empiricist's full satisfaction. CE is, as Rosen has shown, rather an allegedly good compromise between two central empiricist commitments doing justice to both as far as possible.

But is CE a compromise that is good enough to put the empiricist's mind at rest and to provide a stable and convincing position regarding the question of what science is and of what it aims at? We will question this in the next section and ponder a few arguments that have recently been directed against van Fraassen's empiricism.

2 Undermining the Compromise

Alspector-Kelly has posed serious criticism as to the idea that CE is a stable and unrivalled position in accordance with van Fraassen's empiricist project.[6]

4 Rosen (1994), pp. 162f.

5 The term "manifestationalism" is due to Peter Railton (Railton (1990)); also cf. Rosen (1994), p. 161.

6 Alspector-Kelly 2001, especially pp. 416-418.

He maintains that we can conceive of epistemologically weaker positions than CE (but stronger than the already mentioned manifestationalism) which are as suitable for an empiricist as CE:

> We could, for example, believe in the empirical adequacy of the theory only from the moment humans began to make observations to the moment they cease doing so.[7]

This can be reformulated as a thesis about the aim of science as follows (call this thesis "CE-"):

> CE-: Science aims to give us theories which are empirically adequate with respect to the time humans live; and acceptance of a theory involves as belief only that it is empirically adequate with respect to this period.

Obviously, CE- is weaker than CE since it restricts the demand for empirical adequacy to the time humans exist. Furthermore, there seems to be no difference between CE and CE- as regards the criterion of adequacy to science. But if, given the empiricist's commitments to epistemic modesty and adequacy to science, CE- fares just as well as CE with respect to the latter and even better than CE with respect to the former, there is no reason or plausibility left for the empiricist to embrace CE rather than CE-. There may even be positions weaker than CE- that still give credit to the empiricist's admiration for science. In any case, CE proves to be not the most satisfying empiricist philosophy of science in light of epistemologically weaker positions which better fulfill the empiricist's demand for epistemic modesty.[8]

7 Ibid. p. 416.

8 Note that manifestationalism will not do as an empiricist philosophy of science because it is apparently at odds with scientific practice. If we restrict the belief that is involved in the acceptance of a theory to its empirical adequacy to *actually observed* entities (past, present and future) there would no longer be any motivation for scientists to put theories so far confirmed to serious experimental tests. Manifestationalism plainly runs counter to what scientists actually do; for a short illustration of this argument see Rosen (1994), pp. 161f.

Ernan McMullin has recently addressed another problem of van Fraassen's recommendation of CE.[9] According to McMullin, an adherent of CE is on equal epistemological footing as an adherent of scientific realism. A scientific realist usually appeals to some sort of abductive reasoning or inference to the best explanation when it comes to the justification of our beliefs in the existence of certain unobservable entities. As is well known, van Fraassen is very critical of such reasoning. But, so McMullin argues, a proponent of CE is in need of abductive reasoning too, since our belief in the adequacy of scientific theories pertains to many observable but actually unobserved entities.[10] If we infer the existence of observable but definitely unobserved entities such as planets orbiting distant stars, we are in no better epistemological position than a scientific realist who is willing to believe in the existence of electrons in the light of cloud chamber experiments. Van Fraassen, however, dismisses all kinds of abductive reasoning that take the form of inferences to the best explanation.[11] Consequently, we can never know whether a theory is empirically adequate *tout court* or just empirically adequate to the phenomena observed so far.[12] Van Fraassen's appeal to epistemic modesty does not only inflict a selective skepticism with regard to unobservables upon the empiricist, but also leads to an agnostic stance towards many observable entities.

Van Fraassen might reply that all this is correct but that it by no means undermines CE as a plausible empiricist claim about the aim of science. Since CE is not an *epistemological* thesis with regard to our knowledge of observable entities, no inconsistency looms if the empiricist holds on to CE as well as to the refusal of whatever inferences to the best explanation. But here again, one has to take into account that, at least implicitly, CE implies an epistemological claim because it requires us to be epistemically optimistic about the empirical adequacy of certain scientific theories. Wouldn't it be strange to determine the

9 McMullin (2003).

10 Inferences of the sort needed by the constructive empiricist, i.e. inferences from observed to unobserved observables, have been called "horizontal" by Stathis Psillos as opposed to "vertical" inferences from observed to unobservable entities; see Psillos (1996). Psillos' terminology is, however, criticized in McMullin (2003), fn. 6.

11 Cf. Ladyman et al. (1997); in *Laws and Symmetry* van Fraassen even seems to dismiss all kinds of ampliative reasoning; cf. LS, p. 151.

12 See Ladyman et al. (1997) for further clarifications on van Fraassen's critique of the inference to the best explanation.

aim of science as giving us empirically adequate theories, if we never had any conclusive evidence for a theory's being empirically adequate?[13] If we refuse to make any inferences from actually observed entities to observable yet unobserved entities, it seems implausible to seek empirical adequacy at all.

From this it becomes obvious that it is exactly the demand for empirical adequacy that brings in the tension between the empiricist's guidelines of epistemic modesty and adequacy to science. Whereas the former gives rise to a weaker formulation of the aim of science as the one given by CE, the latter inevitably leads to an implicit appeal to the legitimacy of some sort of inference to the best explanation. A manifestationalist doctrine of the aim of science, although serving well the demand for epistemic modesty, would fail to accommodate familiar scientific practices of inferring to observable but unobserved entities. Thus, CE turns out to be not only unstable but rather inconsistent with an overall empiricist approach.

Lastly, we would like to cast some doubts on the adequacy of CE to scientific practice. Even if one grants that CE can be defended as a stable and consistent empiricist claim about the aim of science, it is still questionable whether CE adequately reflects the goals of scientific activity and the implications of theory-acceptance. As we pointed out in section two van Fraassen does not equate the aim of science with what scientists take to be the aim of their professional doings. He rather calls for a philosophical pre-understanding of science that is to be presupposed in order to even distinguish scientific from non-scientific practice. But that doesn't immunize an empiricist approach to science against empirical refutation. Van Fraassen himself ponders over the consequences an empiricist had to face in case "CE [could not] be carried through as an interpretation of science with respect to what we all come to agree on classifying as science" (GRCE, p. 191).

Of course, van Fraassen holds that CE makes good sense of what science is and what scientists do. From the point of view of a constructive empiricist it is precisely the belief that a theory is empirically adequate that is in-

13 McMullin confronts van Fraassen with a similar question when he tries to lay bare the realist requirements of van Fraassen's empiricist approach; McMullin (2003), pp. 472ff.

volved in the acceptance of a theory. Furthermore, pragmatic virtues of theories such as elegance, simplicity or unifying power also play an important role when it comes to the question of choosing between rival theories that are empirically equivalent.[14] It is explanatory success with respect to these pragmatic criteria – however they may be spelled out and weighed against each other – that makes science useful and worthwhile according to an adherent of CE and that enables us to distinguish scientific from non-scientific activity. It is in light of science's various endeavors for pragmatic explanations, usefulness, and success that van Fraassen proposes CE with its focus on empirical adequacy as a promising candidate for the formulation of the aim of science.[15]

However, a scientific realist will instantly reply that a defense of CE along these lines is question-begging. She will argue that it is the very contentious issue of the debate on scientific realism whether the success of scientific theories is essentially tied to their unrestricted truth or solely rests on their empirical adequacy and pragmatic merits. Obviously, it would not count as a conclusive argument if the constructive empiricist praised CE's adequacy to science and its success in light of a notion of success that is intimately related to CE itself.

We cannot further elaborate on this point here. At any rate, it seems most sensible to us to keep epistemological questions as to what we are entitled to believe and the question as to what might adequately be conceived of as the aim of science strictly apart from each other. Surely, van Fraassen will not embrace this line of reasoning, since he maintains that the debate about scientific realism is at bottom a debate about the aim of science. But perhaps we managed to cast some doubt on this idiosyncrasy.

14 With respect to the role of pragmatic virtues for evaluating theories according to CE cf. SI, pp. 87ff.

15 In particular, van Fraassen argues that the attribution of explanatory power to a theory, i.e. the attribution of certain *pragmatic* virtues such as simplicity and so on, includes in part the attribution of *epistemic* virtues, notably empirical adequacy. Therefore, according to CE, the search for useful theories implies the search for empirical adequate theories; cf. SI, pp. 88f.

Conclusion

Van Fraassen's version of empiricism places two constraints on his philosophy of science, namely *epistemic modesty* and *adequacy to science.* Agreeing with Rosen, we interpret CE as a compromise between these two constraints. But as we have tried to show in this paper, there is a strong tension between epistemic modesty and adequacy to science which renders CE an unsatisfying compromise. In our view, serious problems arise because van Fraassen relates epistemic modesty to the observable/unobservable distinction rather than to an observed/observable distinction. Therefore, van Fraassen has to reconsider either his overall picture of empiricism or his philosophy of science, i.e. CE.

References

Alspector-Kelly, Marc (2001): "Should the Empiricist Be a Constructive Empiricist?", *Philosophy of Science* 68, pp. 413-431.

Ladyman, James et al. (1997): "A Defence of van Fraassen's Critique of Abductive Inference", *Philosophical Quarterly* 47, pp. 305-321.

McMullin, Ernan (2003): "Van Fraassen's Unappreciated Realism", *Philosophy of Science* 70, pp. 455-478.

Psillos, Stathis (1996): "On van Fraassen's Critique of Abductive Reasoning", *Philosophical Quarterly* 46, pp. 31-47.

Railton, Peter (1990): "Explanation and Metaphysical Controversy", *Minnesota Studies in the Philosophy of Science* XIII, pp. 220-252.

Rosen, Gideon (1994): "What is Constructive Empiricism?", *Philosophical Studies* 74, pp. 143-178.

EXPERIENCE BECOMING FULLY LITERATE

Van Fraassen on the Verge of Constructivism

Marie Kaiser, Raja Rosenhagen, Christian Suhm

Abstract: The aim of this paper is to scrutinize Bas van Fraassen's concept of observation in light of its role for constructive empiricism on the one hand and van Fraassen's recent considerations on the notion of experience on the other. In particular, we show that a dilemma emerges to the effect that van Fraassen is forced to accept skeptical consequences blatantly at odds with constructive empiricism and its restatement of the aim of science. We suggest that the only way out for van Fraassen involves giving up his realistic construal of observability and taking sides with constructivism.

Keywords: observation, observable/unobservable distinction, realism, constructivism, theory-dependence

INTRODUCTION

The observable/unobservable distinction, realistically construed, lies at the very heart of van Fraassen's constructive empiricism. The aim of this paper is to approach it by taking a close look at van Fraassen's concept of observation. We will argue that if van Fraassen's most recent writings about "literate experience" (LE, p. 331)[1], especially his remarks on the status of observation reports and his general a-metaphysical stance, are taken into account, his realistic interpretation of the observable/unobservable distinction paves the road for inconsistency. In particular, we will show that a dilemma emerges to the

1 Our analysis of van Fraassen's constructivist likings will, to a considerable part, rest on the parallel between interpreting a text and experiencing nature he draws in LE.

effect that van Fraassen is forced to accept skeptical consequences blatantly at odds with constructive empiricism and its restatement of the aim of science. Finally, we will suggest that the only way out for van Fraassen involves giving up his realistic construal of observability and, thus, taking sides with constructivism.

1 The Concept of Observation

The first task will be to find out what it is that van Fraassen alludes to by using the terms 'observation' or 'experience'.[2] In his most recent writings, van Fraassen explicitly criticizes concepts of observation which accommodate metaphysical realism. According to van Fraassen, an advocate of metaphysical realism claims that, while observing, one is able to catch a glimpse of what the structure of nature is really like (LE, pp. 347f.), i.e. of "properties, attributes, Universals, Relations – in short, [of the] real structure present in the things" (LE, p. 347) themselves which are completely independent of any judging and classifying activity of the observer.

Van Fraassen challenges such a view. He thinks that all natural phenomena are "received as symbols, words or sentences in a language, of which we already have some pre-understanding" (LE, p. 353). Every observation or experience we make involves a judgment about the structure of nature that is couched in our own language. (LE, p. 353) What we characterize as the structure of nature is not independent of the observer's "creative activity" (LE, p. 348) and interpretation, as the language she uses is highly theory-infected. Consequently, structure is attributed to nature whenever we describe it via our classifications and observation reports. (LE, p. 350) In the following passage van Fraassen underlines this consideration by drawing a parallel between discerning structure in nature and understanding a text:

> As for us, we discern structure in nature; but the structure we discern there, we discern in the same way as we discern a story when looking at

2 Van Fraassen takes it that ""observation" is the code for scientifically relevant experience" (LE, p. 355).

> ink marks on a page. We read it initially in the language we already have [...] [and based on those] theories with which that language was already infected at our birth. (LE, p. 354)

It is exactly in the light of this parallel that van Fraassen's demand for "literate experience" (LE, p. 331) makes sense. As there is always leeway for the interpretation of a literary text, though some readings will count as cases of overinterpretation, 'reading' nature is not regimented by some external structure independent of us, but rather becomes literate by learning a particular language and by adopting a theoretical tradition. (LE, pp. 348ff.)[3]

Another aspect central to van Fraassen's conception of observation, namely the distinction between *observing* and *observing that*, is illustrated by a short fictional story in *The Scientific Image* (SI, p. 15): Observer B1, who has been educated as a member of the modern 20th century, knows everything about tennis and is familiar with the term 'tennis ball'. Imagine that B1 stands in the relation of observing with an entity X and that she points at the entity and gives the following observation report: 'This is a tennis ball'.[4] Observer B2, who is a member of the Stone Age people, has never heard anything of a game called 'tennis' nor does she know what the term 'tennis ball' refers to. She will probably make a completely different observation report, when she stands in the relation of observing to X. For instance, she might report something like 'This is yellow and not edible' or something along those lines.[5] If two observers B1 and B2 stand in the relation of observing to an entity X, it does apparently not follow that both will automatically frame the same observation report. Depending on their different background theories and the concepts they rely on, depending on the language game they live and breathe in and from which they cannot escape, both observers will express different statements.

3 The details of van Fraassen's comparison in LE between text and nature on the one hand, and interpretation and experience on the other, cannot be dealt with in this paper.

4 It goes without saying that this observation report is totally correct and in accordance with the classifications she and her contemporary language-users use.

5 Here, the same as in the previous footnote holds. Depending on her ontological commitments and her practical interests, she might even say something like 'Look, small sun-like roundness' or 'non-edible instantiation of yellowness'.

The observation *that* an observed entity is actually a tennis ball as well as the expression of the corresponding observation report in which the term 'tennis ball' occurs can only be made by someone who is familiar with the game of tennis. Both presuppose a background theory of tennis and mastery of its central concepts. But according to van Fraassen, the observation of the tennis ball, i.e. the mere fact that a relation of observing between an observer and a particular entity X obtains, is independent of the observer's language and theories. This point which implies a realistic understanding of the property of being observable will be subjected to further analysis in the third section of this paper. Even if it seems that B1 and B2 could agree on some basic facts about the entity perceived – its being yellow or its being round-shaped – the observers' possible agreement does only reflect some degree of similarity of the language games they play. Nothing like a neutral basic perception is involved and nothing follows from a possible similarity of the observers' language games for the real structure of the entity in question.

Accordingly, van Fraassen claims that the relation between the *content* of an observation report and the *conditions* of observing is neither necessary nor a priori. (VC, pp. 15, 17) Rather, he construes it as a highly reliable sort of measuring which has been established by some (however specified) process of conditioning. (VC, pp. 15, 17) However, observation reports or judgments "are not epistemically secure foundations" (VC, p. 20), they are "full of empirical risk" (VC, p. 20). They do not warrant objective certainty, but only confer a high probability that certain conditions of observing obtain – whatever those may be – to which the observer has been conditioned to react in a specific way. For instance, if an observer reports 'I see a tennis ball', there is a high probability that the kind of conditions obtain, to which the observer has been conditioned to react with this report. Again, nothing more is implied about the entity observed. The content of the statement 'I see a tennis ball' has no a priori link whatsoever to what the entity observed is really like. The entity in the real world and its properties could well have differed from what the observer reported it to be like. The fact that the observer states an observation report only signalizes that some observable entity was probably present to him and that the circumstances were probably 'just right', so that the relation of observing was established. Nothing about the report implies infallibility of the observer's judgment or understanding, though. (ES, p. 136)

As far as our observations of trees, tables, tennis balls, and the like are concerned, van Fraassen apparently holds that we have pragmatic reasons for being epistemically optimistic, particularly since "we can only start from where we are". (MM, p. 480) From a philosophical perspective which takes van Fraassen's general remarks about observation into account, though, even reports about familiar middle-sized objects cannot refer to nature as being independent of us but only to nature as it is represented by us. However, van Fraassen does not take his position to be a "debilitating form of skepticism", but rather as a description of our "actual situation", our "human condition", from which we cannot escape. (ES, p. 133)

The seemingly all-pervading theory- and language-dependence to the contrary, van Fraassen explicitly allows for "elements that are not text at all" (ES, p. 136), something that "is 'really going on'" (WE, p. 133), "events which happen to us" (ES, p. 134), „the facts themselves“ (LE, p. 354) that exist independent of our theories and our language. In his paper *Literate Experience* he makes that very explicit, claiming that his position does not amount to subjective idealism:

> Let us begin by asserting unequivocally that what nature is like does not depend on what we think, or how we view it, or even on our existence at all. (LE, p. 352)
>
> What nature is like does not depend on what our experience or representation of nature is like. (LE, p. 354)

It seems that van Fraassen denies that we have any kind of epistemic access to structural elements of nature that are conceptually independent of us. Whatever structure we come to discern in nature can only be conceived of as something we attribute to nature in describing what happens to us. Still, van Fraassen does not deny the very existence of an independent nature as such, as he unambiguously presupposes the existence of entities independent of us, entities with which we can – the right circumstances being actual – stand in the relation of observing.

2 Observability Realistically Construed

As has already been noted, van Fraassen opposes metaphysical claims such as metaphysical realism. He rejects forms of ontology according to which structures in nature are postulated as independent of us.[6] Only theory- and language-dependent phenomena should, so he argues, be accepted as real, whereas any ascriptions of structure to nature could well be seen as "a unifying myth to illuminate our path". (WE, p. 133) The aim of this section is to show that van Fraassen's rebellion against metaphysical postulates as to the existence of structure in nature does not correspond to his claim that observability is a property[7] entities have independent of our background theories and our language. In our view, such a claim rests on a sort of restricted metaphysical realism.

More to the point: Van Fraassen presupposes the existence of entities which may or may not have the property of being observable for us. Moreover, their existence is independent of the language game we play and independent of our background theories:

> What can be observed, and what there really is to be observed, is a matter of fact – it is not theory-, mind-, or language-dependent, but is there regardless of whether we even so much as pay attention to it. (LE, p. 355)

Van Fraassen's realism with respect to observability is rather an ontological than an epistemological claim. An observer may not only be mistaken about the adequacy of his observation reports as far as their contents are concerned

6 This becomes also very much explicit in *The Empirical Stance*: "As I see it, the targets [of empiricist critique] are forms of metaphysics that (a) give absolute primacy to demands for explanation and (b) are satisfied with explanations-by-postulate, that is, explanations that postulate the reality of certain entities or aspects of the world not already evident in experience." (ES, p. 37)

7 Strictly speaking, observability is a relation of at least three relata: an entity X, an observer B (or rather an epistemic community E), and certain circumstances (C1, C2, …, Cn). Moreover, as the property of observability is not permanently manifest it seems appropriate to classify it as a dispositional property. Anyway, these considerations can be neglected in the course of this paper.

(MM, p. 484; SP, p. 524; ES, p. 136), but can also err on whether she actually observes an entity or not.

Of course, observers usually have clear opinions about whether certain entities are observable (trees, tables, tennis balls, mountains, and the like) or not (electrons, leptons, propositions, whatever you like). We as observers, thus, have at least a tentative answer to the question as to how the observable/unobservable-distinction works. But this, again, "depends on the historical character of the language" and is "heavily perspectival" (VC, p. 20):

> The question of what there is to be observed is a question which in each of our mouths takes on the meaning of the language in which we live and breathe and have our being. (LE, p. 355)

So there are two things we have to distinguish: On the one hand, van Fraassen claims that our *opinions* about the observability of entities (for us) depend on the theories and language we have. On the other hand, he holds that the *property* of being observable for us is both theory- and language-independent.

But here we come to realize a striking tension between van Fraassen's realism concerning observability and his rejection of language- and theory-independent structures in nature. Obviously, the former implies the existence of a certain structure in nature. A realistic attitude towards observability and observation draws on distinctions between different types of entities, e.g. observables and unobservables or observers and non-observers.[8] Furthermore, there are circumstances such that if an observable entity is present to an observer under those circumstances, then she observes it. And all this is regarded as being independent of any theory or language whatsoever.

In the light of what has been said regarding van Fraassen's dismissal of metaphysical realism such realistic claims about structural properties of the world sound quite surprising. Inferring from classifications we make that "there is in the things classified a real basis for demarcation" (LE, p. 347), i.e., that there is a kind of structure in nature which is independent of us, seems to

8 Even if it is claimed that there are only observable, though realistically understood, entities in the world, to say so is to attribute structure to a language- and theory-independent nature since observable entities at least differ numerically from each other.

be the same fallacy van Fraassen criticizes as the fundamental error of the metaphysical realist. Why then, we ask, should it be warranted to make an exception of observability and of observation? Why should the claim that entities differ with regard to the property of being observable and with regard to the relation of observation fare any better than all the other claims of the metaphysical realist?

3 RUNNING INTO A DILEMMA

In the preceding section we have shown that van Fraassen attributes a theory-independent structure to nature, at least with respect to the distinction between its observable and unobservable parts. Thereby, he seems to make the same move as does the metaphysical realist who regards the truth of theoretical classifications as being grounded in theory-independent, real structures in nature. But whereas van Fraassen finds the metaphysical realist guilty of making unwarranted substantial postulates and of reifying structures, he claims for himself to "walk[…] a fine line" (LE, p. 355) between realism as regards observability on the one hand, and some sort of constructivism as regards the structure of nature on the other. We take this simply to be a euphemism for an internal inconsistency in van Fraassen's conception of experience. But let us suppose, for the sake of the argument, that van Fraassen's realism regarding observability can be consistently held together with an assimilation of experiencing nature to interpreting literary texts. Even if so much is granted, another serious problem arises as to whether we can ever have any knowledge[9] about what is observable in nature.

Van Fraassen's realistic conception of observability is part and parcel of constructive empiricism in that it gives rise to an epistemically relevant distinction between an observable and an unobservable part of nature. Therefore, it relies on empirical adequacy as a plausible aim of science. Van Fraassen, as we shall assume, will not give up this conception lightly, but will try to

9 In accordance with the standard view we regard knowledge as justified true belief. We do not, however, intend to introduce any elaborate theory of knowledge or conception of justification here.

reconcile it with his more recent considerations on the language- and theory-dependence of structure. But it is exactly in the light of this synthesis that worries about running into a dilemmatic scenario emerge. If observability is to be interpreted as ontologically realistic, i.e. as being independent of language, theories, or the human mind, two epistemic standpoints seem to be possible. Either van Fraassen remains skeptical about our epistemic access to the property of being observable and thereby neglects that we will ever be in a position to know that certain things are observable. Or he adopts a more or less optimistic stance towards our ability to ascertain the observability of things in nature – better and more comprehensively in the course of scientific progress.

The skeptical option makes up the first horn of the dilemma. The motivation for adopting a skeptical attitude towards observability may be taken to be expressed in van Fraassen's claim that structure is not something to be attributed to reality in itself, but something that is due to our classifications and concepts. As was shown in section three, the distinction between an observable and an unobservable part in nature can undoubtedly be subsumed under the notion of structure. Consequently, the ascription of observability to particular parts of nature cannot be conceived of as the result of a discovery of a language- or theory-independent property. So it seems that there is no reason for epistemic optimism with regard to observability and observation as objective structural elements of reality. Moreover, it seems to be impossible to enter the constructive empiricist's "hermeneutic circle" (SI, p. 57) between tentative beliefs about observability and future scientific findings about it at all. If in principle there is no warrant that at least some objects are clear cases of observable entities it makes no sense to hope for further scientific results as to the question where the line between observable and unobservable things in nature has to be drawn. A skeptical attitude towards observability and observation seems to be unavoidable, if one assumes that any structure we ascribe to reality has to be regarded as language- and theory-dependent.[10]

10 From a pragmatic point of view there may be, of course, no choice but to enter the hermeneutic circle of scientific progress. We can only start from where we are, so much can be granted. The point is that there is no reason to believe that by means of the hermeneutic circle we are brought any step nearer to a description of the true observable/unobservable distinction.

However, acceptance of this skeptical consequence will inevitably erode the very basis of van Fraassen's constructive empiricism. To claim that it is the aim of science to give us theories that are empirically adequate, and to ground the notion of empirical adequacy on an objective distinction between the observable and the unobservable, makes sense only on the assumption that we have knowledge of the observability of at least some objects. What plausibility could one claim for reconstructing science as an activity aiming at the adequate description of observable phenomena, if there were no pieces of knowledge at all about observability?

By conceding that there is such knowledge van Fraassen takes the second horn of the dilemma. Let us grant that by future scientific theories we will ascertain more detailed information about the functioning of human sense organs and, thereby, will learn more about what is observable for us. Whatever these theories will look like, they will necessarily include ascriptions of structure to certain parts of reality, namely to the physiological make-up of human beings relevant to the observation of external objects. Here again, one has to take into account van Fraassen's considerations on the theory-dependence of any structure we ascribe to reality. Scientific theories, including those which will give us the precise structure of sense organs, cannot be regarded as detectors of theory-independent structures of reality. From this it follows that theory-mediated knowledge of the borders of observability cannot be counted as knowledge of a theory-independent observable/unobservable distinction in nature. According to van Fraassen, observation reports, being adduced to confirm or corroborate theories, themselves turn out to be theory-dependent classifications and structure ascriptions. So, unfortunately, we are at last thrown back to the first horn of the dilemma, namely to a skeptical attitude towards observability. And, as was already argued, this attitude is inappropriate to van Fraassen's anti-realist approach in the philosophy of science.

Whatever epistemological point of view van Fraassen wishes to take with respect to observability construed realistically, in either case he seems to be forced to accept skeptical consequences blatantly at odds with constructive empiricism and its restatement of the aim of science.

Let us take stock. If the preceding analyses of van Fraassen's concepts of observability and observation are correct, he is faced with a serious internal tension, or even inconsistency, in his overall account of experience and its importance for determining the aim of science. We suspect that it is van Fraassen's strong loyalty to the project of empiricism and parts of its history, especially to the search for a fundament of all knowledge in experience, which makes him come to a purportedly sustainable compromise. On the one hand he readily accepts a nearly all-embracing theory- and language-dependence of experience, on the other he clings to a realistic understanding of observability and observation as the cornerstones of empiricism. But if this compromise leads to inconsistency, wouldn't it be more promising for van Fraassen to leave his "fine line" and take sides with constructivism altogether? Perhaps experience will not become fully literate until it is realized that observability is due to classifications made by us rather than a structure in nature itself.

INDEXICAL TRUTH AND ANTI-METAPHYSICAL INCLINATIONS

Getting Rid of the Remnants of Realism

Raja Rosenhagen

Abstract: In this paper a close look is taken at van Fraassen's use of the concept of truth. It is shown that the rather deflationist understanding of the term in his more recent publications differs considerably from the one referred to in his earlier writings, where the truth of a scientific theory is construed as its correspondence to the world. As will be argued, his more recent remarks call for a re-evaluation of the difference between scientific realism and constructive empiricism and force him – for the sake of consistency – to give up his realist commitments regarding the world and the observable.

Keywords: constructive empiricism, truth, semantic view, scientific realism, scientific theories

INTRODUCTION

The notion 'truth' has long time been subject to considerable debate in philosophy. In the writings of van Fraassen the terms 'true' and 'truth' appear frequently. It seems, though, that on different occasions of its use van Fraassen refers to different concepts respectively.

In some of his earlier writings the term 'truth' has a quite substantial ring to it; truth of a scientific theory, so it seems, is construed as correspondence of that theory to the world, i.e. to facts, things, events, and processes in the world behind the phenomena. The aim of the first section of this paper will be to show van Fraassen's extensive use of such a substantial concept of truth.

At other places, mostly in his more recent publications, van Fraassen uses an idiosyncratic version of a non-substantial concept of truth. Here the notion of truth is taken to be tacitly indexical to our own language. Thus, truth is no longer understood as correspondence between theories and the world as such. Rather, it is a relation between scientific theories and statements in which *we* describe the world as it is represented *by us*. This understanding of the term 'truth' will be dealt with in the second section of this paper.

In the third section we will show that the two readings of 'true' are incompatible. We will suggest that if van Fraassen's claims in his more recent writings are to be taken seriously then he must also give up the last remnants of realism in his theory: the realism concerning the property of being observable and the idea that there exists a causally and conceptually mind-independent world. We conclude that being forced to do so van Fraassen – his intentions to the contrary – lands himself in idealism or pragmatism.

1 TRUTH AS CORRESPONDENCE TO THE REAL WORLD

Let us first take a look at how truth is defined in what probably counts as the most influential piece of van Fraassen's early writings: *The Scientific Image*. In *The Scientific Image* van Fraassen develops his constructive empiricism as an alternative to scientific realism. Both of these philosophical positions are taken to involve distinct answers to two questions: a) 'what is the aim of science?' and b) 'what beliefs are involved in accepting a scientific theory'. Scientific realism is characterized as embracing the statement that "*Science aims to give us, in its theories, a literally true story of what the world is like; and acceptance of a scientific theory involves the belief that it is true.*" (SI, p. 8, emphasis by van Fraassen) Constructive empiricists advocate that "*Science aims to give us theories which are empirically adequate; and acceptance of a theory involves as belief only that it is empirically adequate.*" (SI, p. 12, emphasis by van Fraassen)

The concept of truth plays no doubt a quite important role both in scientific realism and van Fraassen's constructive empiricism as it is well known that the term 'empirically adequate' is defined as 'true regarding the observable'. We might expect of van Fraassen that he provide us with a detailed account of what he has in mind, when truth is referred to. Surprisingly, this is not so. Instead, some rather sketchy remarks are scattered all over the book.[1] However, our task shall now be to collect these remarks and to try to bring them into a coherent picture.

In the introduction of *The Scientific Image* 'being true' is equated with "one relation a theory may have to the world" (SI, p. 3) and van Fraassen asserts that a theory stands in that relation to the world if it gives "a true account of the facts" (SI, p. 3).[2] Thus, truth is explicitly described as a relation which obtains between theory and world, between theory and facts.[3] When van Fraassen ponders just what scientific realism is, a true theory is characterized as giving a picture of the world which is "faithful in its details, and [thus, if the theory is true,] the entities postulated in science really exist" (SI, p. 7). A scientific theory is "a story about what there really is" (SI, p. 7). What makes that story true or false "is something external – that is to say, it is not (in general) our sense data, actual or potential, or the structure of our minds, or our lan-

1 It might be objected that those remarks – at least not all of them – can not just be used as evidence for what van Fraassen takes to be an appropriate concept of truth. The problem is that at least some of the statements in which more detailed information are offered about what truth is supposed to be are not statements of van Fraassen himself, but statements he attributes to or quotes from scientific realists. But then, van Fraassen uses the word 'true' without demur, without putting any additional constraints on its usage. It is used rather freely, for example when he gives his own account of what empirical adequacy is. We shall therefore be justified to assume that van Fraassen's views and those he ascribes to his philosophical opponents do not differ much as far as truth is concerned.

2 This assertion is a very valuable one, as it is not attributed to scientific realists; it is a statement van Fraassen offers as his own.

3 Of course, we could again press the statement further and ask questions as 'what does the term <world> denote here?', 'what are facts and what ontological status do they have?', and the like. But maybe we should not be so painstakingly hard to please. Let us take for granted, at least for now, that there was an ordinary use of those words when van Fraassen wrote *The Scientific Image* and let us furthermore assume that this use brought with it the commonsensical understanding that 'world' and 'facts' denote something causally and conceptually independent from us.

guage, etc." (SI, p. 8)[4] This last quotation is particularly interesting, as it more precisely states what the status of the entities in the world is, the 'truth-makers', if you wish. They are 'something external' and emphatically *not* dependent on our language or on the structure of our minds.

Van Fraassen is an adherent of the semantic view of scientific theories. A naïve formula which characterizes that view is: 'theories are families of models'.[5] Due to the claim that to present a scientific theory is to identify a family of its models it seems at least prima facie plausible to claim that "if the theory as such, is to be identified with anything at all – if theories are to be reified – then a theory should be identified with its class of models." (LS, p. 222) The problem with this naïve formula is, however, that models are not the kind of things about which we would say that they are true or false. Van Fraassen is well aware of that, too. In a reply to Pérez Ransanz he admits that "a theory must be the sort of thing that *can* be true or false" (OQI, p. 21), thus, theories have to include an element which can be the "object of epistemic or at least doxastic attitudes" (SAST, p. 106). Following Ronald Giere's idea, van Fraassen identifies theories in two steps. By means of a so-called theoretical definition the class of models belonging to the theory is defined, the theoretical hypothesis is "the proposition that certain real entities in the world belong to this class" (OQI, p. 23).[6] The latter, so we should conclude, is the object of our doxastic attitudes we have been looking for. If a theory is said to be true that is to say that its theoretical hypothesis is.

What can we conclude about the concept of truth so far brought to light? First, we note that the things that can be called 'true' or 'false' are theories or – to be more precise – the respective theoretical hypotheses, i.e. propositions. If we assert a certain theory to be true, we say that it has among its models "a model which is a faithful replica, in all detail, of our world" (SI, p. 68). Being true for a theory is to stand in a certain relation to the world. If we give in our theory an appropriate account on 'what there really is' in the world, then our theory is true. The world referred to in our true theories is

4 Quoting Dummett (1978), p. 146 and pp. 358-61.

5 This is the slogan which is found in a big part of the literature pertaining to the semantic view. See for example Suppe (2000), p. 105, Suárez (1999), p. 75, Chakravartty (2001), p. 325 and Fine (2001), p. 113.

6 See also SAST, pp. 110f. and LS, p. 222.

populated with entities that really exist and which do so (at least in part) causally and conceptually independent of us. After so much has been said, we are no longer surprised when van Fraassen offers us the final clue and reveals that he subscribes to a correspondence theory of truth: "I would still identify truth of a theory with the condition that there is an exact correspondence between reality and one of its [i.e. the theory's] models." (SI, p. 197)

The purpose of this first section has been served. Van Fraassen, sharing the basic concept of 'truth' with most of his philosophical opponents, construes truth as correspondence of a theory (however you prefer to picture it) to the world. The main difference between the position scientific realists putatively hold and the one that is advocated by constructive empiricists is a difference in opinion about which parts of the scientific theories that science aims at are true so construed. Whereas the scientific realist claims that science aims at theories which are true *tout court*, the constructive empiricist sees the aim of science in providing theories that are empirically adequate, that is, true only "with respect to the observable phenomena" (cf. SAST, p. 107).[7]

2 Truth as Indexical

To understand the concept of truth that is used in van Fraassen's more recent writings, we will have to take a little detour: One result that has been achieved in the preceding section is that a theory should be reckoned empirically adequate if it is true about the observable things and events in the world. Let us examine another statement about what empirical adequacy of a theory is: It says that "the theory is empirically adequate if it has some model such that all appearances are isomorphic to empirical substructures of that model." (SI, p. 64)

In this passage it is neither phenomena, nor observables, but rather appearances that stand in the relation to the theory. Appearances are then intro-

7 This view is still held by van Fraassen today, as can be seen in one of his most recent publications, where theories are claimed to be empirically adequate if the "observable part of nature fits into some model which is in accord with" that given theories (MM, p. 483).

duced as "structures which can be described in experimental and measurement reports" (SI, p. 64). But what are these structures, then? Let us delay the answer to that question for a moment and take a look at some general thoughts van Fraassen conveys in his more recent writings. In *The Empirical Stance* van Fraassen clearly expresses his dislike for metaphysics. He characterizes the story of empiricism as "a story full of rebellion against [...] the metaphysicians" (ES, p. 36), especially against

> forms of metaphysics that (a) give absolute primacy to demands for explanation and (b) are satisfied with explanations by postulate, that is, explanations that postulate the reality of certain entities or aspects of the world not already evident in experience. (ES, p. 37)

In his essay "Literate Experience" van Fraassen compares experience and the attribution of structure to nature to the activity of reading and interpreting a text. As a reader of a text has to become literate in order to understand it so does experience. Thus, "Literate Experience equals reading the Book of Nature" (LE, p. 346). In good empiricist tradition van Fraassen once more attacks the metaphysical realist. He claims that "there is a sense of 'attributing structure'" to nature according to which "to say that nature resists certain forms of reading, of literate experience, is to attribute properties, characteristics, and structure. Metaphysical realism slips from this minimalist sense into substantive postulates" (LE, p. 350). Thus, if we insist "that the structure [in nature] is there independently of any judging, classifying or 'reading' activity" (LE, p. 347), we become the sort of metaphysical realist that van Fraassen opposes. We must not think that "there is in the things classified some real basis for demarcation [...] [and that this] basis must be [...] properties, attributes, Universals, Relations – in short, real structure present in the things" (LE, p. 347).

Let us again stress what van Fraassen says here: We do not – so van Fraassen's claims – know anything about the real structure of the world.[8] Ra-

8 There is of course an exception, as van Fraassen claims that the observable/unobservable distinction is theory-neutral. In another paper of this volume it is argued that this view cannot be consistently upheld (cf. Kaiser, Rosenhagen and Suhm, this volume). We will come back to that point later, though.

ther, structure is something we attribute to nature whenever we describe it. This fact has important implications for the notion of truth. An example van Fraassen offers may serve to illustrate this: If we state a sentence like 'Snow is white', then we think that this sentence is true iff snow is white. But van Fraassen seems to suggest that this tells us nothing about the structure of the world itself. It is not necessary to believe that there is some (mind-independent) entity like snow in the world, which has the (mind-independent) property of being white. In our language snow is something that has the property of being white. We have no choice but to bestow an "indispensable reliance on our understanding of our own language" (ES, p. 132). We cannot step out of that understanding, dealing "with our language as if it were an alien syntax" (SP, p. 520), trying to "think of our understanding or interpretation as a further text [...] that we could then believe or disbelieve, doubt or dispute." (ES, p. 132)

Let us see what this means for the understanding of the concept of truth. If we use the notion 'true' – so van Fraassen claims – then

> it [i.e. the notion 'true'] is indexical – tacitly indexical. The tacit indexical reference is to our language. The criteria for understanding of our own language express themselves in pragmatic tautologies. (SP, pp. 520f.)

Van Fraassen offers an example: He asserts that the term 'cat' denotes cats. While this is certainly true, its being so has a simple explanation: Our language just works that way. The fact that 'cat' denotes cats is "undeniable by me if I acknowledge "cat" to be a word in my language." (SP, p. 521) Stating it is stating the obvious, it is nothing but a pragmatic tautology.

Let us end this section by looking again at empirical adequacy: Empirical adequacy is truth regarding the observable phenomena. The observable phenomena are present to us only as appearances, via our observation judgments and descriptions. Moreover, in those descriptions we attribute structure to the world, but we are not warranted in inferring from our attribution practices to the claim that there is a real basis for our structural attributions in the world itself. Finally, a proposition's being true is only being tacitly indexical to our own language. It follows that scientific theories which are empirically adequate and thus true regarding the observable phenomena are not necessarily related to the world at all. For, to say that a scientific theory is true is to say that its theoretical hypothesis is undeniable by us. But even if this were so, then it would only be a reflection of how our language works. We would not be allowed to infer anything whatsoever about the world itself.

3 Remnants of Realism – Observables in the Mind-Independent World

In the last two sections some effort has been made to show that the notion 'truth' is used in different ways by van Fraassen. In the earlier writings truth is taken to be correspondence, in later writings as tacitly indexical to our own language. Both views seem to be incompatible. When we say that a theory (or some part of it) is true we can only mean one thing: Either that it stands in a relation to the world, which is causally and conceptually independent of us – that is the reading we found proliferating in *The Scientific Image* – or that it stands in relation to the world as described by us – this reading has been suggested by van Fraassen's more recent writings.

But is it not possible that both relations somehow coincide, if our description of the world as described by us matches the world as it really is? We might feel that van Fraassen could agree. He might want to say that – of course – to stick to an understanding of truth-for-us as a non-substantial notion on the one hand does allow that we use a second, more substantial concept of truth. We should just keep in mind that we can never know if that substantial relation obtains or not, because the world is only available to us via our description of it. Thus, even if truth in the stronger, that is, substantial sense of it, might possibly obtain, that would be completely out of our epistemic reach.

Whereas such an answer seems prima facie possible, van Fraassen does not seem to go for it. For him "questions of truth make sense exactly and only to the extent that we have words to describe what things are like" (SP, p. 529). As we (trivially) cannot describe the world as it is independent from our description, we cannot employ a notion of truth that is construed as correspondence to the causally and conceptually independent world – as it doesn't make sense. One might even claim that the notion 'causally and conceptually independent world' is unintelligible (as some pragmatists do).

Taking in account the analyses of the preceding two sections, the difference between the position of the scientific realist as depicted by van Fraassen in *The Scientific Image* and the position of a constructive empiricist cannot be construed as simply amounting to a difference of opinion about what part of the scientific theories that science aims at is true, substantially understood. The differences run much deeper, as for the scientific realist, theories are about the world and truth is correspondence. For the constructive empiricist, theories are not about the world. Rather, they are just about the world as it is described by us. Those descriptions, however, do not tell us anything about the real structure of the world – if there is any, that is – because the fact that we attribute structure to nature does not imply that there is any basis in the world that warrants that attribution. Theories that are empirically adequate are true in a tacitly indexical sense. They tell us things we cannot – using our own language – consistently deny.

We finally want to elaborate on two problematic claims: a) van Fraassen's claim that there is a causally and conceptually mind-independent world and b) his claim that the property of being observable has to be construed realistically. The first claim is made very much explicit in "Literate Experience", when van Fraassen rejects subjective idealism:

> Let us begin by asserting unequivocally that what nature is like does not depend on what we think, or how we view it, or even on our existence at all. (LE, p. 352)

The second claim is constantly repeated in his writings, we shall add only one token here:

> What can be observed, and what there really is to be observed, is a matter of fact – it is not theory-, mind-, or language-dependent, but is there regardless of whether we even so much as pay attention to it. (LE, p. 355)

We will begin with the first claim. When will such a claim be true? If we take van Fraassen by his word, the notion 'true' is elliptic, i.e. tacitly indexical and the indexical reference is to the language in which the sentence is uttered. And as the "criteria for understanding of our own language express themselves in pragmatic tautologies" (SP, p. 521) we may infer that the sentence 'what nature is like does not depend on what we think, or how we view it, or even on our existence at all' is true exactly if what it says is a truism in our language, something which is undeniable by us. Whether we regard it as such will depend on what we believe and on what philosophical theories infect the initial account we give of what we describe as happenings that happen to us. The expression 'what nature is like, independent from us' is just another piece of theory, nothing more. Whatever it is, the first claim, so construed, does just not seem to be true. From van Fraassen's perspective, it cannot be substantially true anyway. And as there have been at least some constructivists, idealists and maybe pragmatists that have denied it, it cannot be true in the indexical sense either, as it is not a truism in our language.[9]

The same strategy can be applied to the second claim: The sentence 'What can be observed, and what there really is to be observed, is a matter of fact – it is not theory-, mind-, or language-dependent' is true iff what is expressed in that sentence is something we cannot deny. To state it is then stating the obvious – a pragmatic tautology. It cannot be a metaphysical claim; it is – once more – just another piece of theory. And as it can be denied by idealists and constructivists, it cannot be true in the indexical sense either. Thus, the property of being observable should better not be construed in a realistic manner.

We conclude that if we rely on van Fraassen's more recent statements about truth, the substantial reading of 'true' we have suggested in the first section is rendered unintelligible. Truth, construed as correspondence of a theory to the world as it is, independent of us, collapses into truth as a relation between what we say in the theoretical hypothesis and what we use to say when

9 Maybe van Fraassen wants to claim that idealists do in fact speak another language than he does. We take this to be a quite unsatisfying answer, though. It does not seem to be a philosophically interesting way of dealing with others' arguments just by pointing out that what they say is not intelligible in one's own language and then leaving it like that.

we describe what happens to us. The concept of a world behind the phenomena and the concept of a realistic property of being observable become just other pieces of theory. If, however, van Fraassen still wants to claim the existence of an independent world and of a theory-neutral property, he faces the problem that such a claim is – according to his recent claims – simply false, as it is not a truism in our language. It could only be made true (or maybe even intelligible) by adopting a different concept of truth or by allowing for more metaphysical realism, both being moves that van Fraassen is not willing to make. Thus, in order to stay in line with his empiricist anti-metaphysical and with his recent deflationist inclinations, we suggest that van Fraassen would do best to abandon those last remnants of realism, to give up on the mind-independent world and side with idealism or pragmatism.

REFERENCES

Chakravartty, Anjan (2001): "The Semantic or Model-Theoretic View of Theories and Scientific Realism", *Synthese* 127, pp. 325-345.

Dummett, Michael (1978): *Truth and Other Enigmas.* Cambridge, Mass.: Harvard University Press.

Fine, Arthur (2001): "The Scientific Image Twenty Years Later", *Philosophical Studies* 106, pp. 107-122.

Suárez, Mauricio (1999): "Theories, Models, and Representations", in Magnani, Nersessian and Thagard (eds.): *Model-Based Reasoning in Scientific Discovery.* Dordrecht: Kluwer 1999, pp. 75-83.

Suppe, Frederick (2000): "Understanding Scientific Theories: An Assessment of Developments, 1969-1998", *Philosophy of Science* 67 (Supplement), Proceedings of the 1998 Biennial Meetings of the Philosophy of Science Association, Part II: Symposia Papers (Sep. 2000), pp. 102-115.

THERE'S LIFE IN THE OLD DOG YET!

Van Fraassen and the death of metaphysics[1]

Sebastian Muders, Matthias Pohl

Abstract: Van Fraassen argues that contemporary metaphysics should be declared dead because it a) does not treat given subjects of significance but rather simulacra, b) does not refer to experience like the natural sciences and c) founds on inference to the best explanation but cannot justify this risk-taking pursuit of truth. We respond ad a) that metaphysical concepts like "the world" show a sufficient similarity and thus substantial significance to our everyday concepts, ad b) that experience is one of the most important sources for metaphysical arguments, as we can see on arguments concerning the existence of God like the argument from design, ad c) that we rely heavily in our everyday thinking and acting on metaphysical ideas.

Keywords: metaphysics, metaphysical concepts, theory-choice

INTRODUCTION

"There's no tonic like reading your own obituary" an analytic metaphysician would probably utter, learning that within 30 pages of argumentation[2] her complete enterprise is declared dead (cf. ES, p. 1). Three points are supposed to do the job: analytic metaphysics

1. does not treat given subjects of significance but rather simulacra;
2. unlike other sciences it does not refer to experience and,

1 We would like to express our deep gratitude to Andreas Hüttemann, who helped us with interesting discussions and his countless advices to write this paper.

2 In this paper we are mainly referring to the first chapter of ES.

3. finally, it founds on inference to the best explanation but cannot justify this risk-taking pursuit of truth.

The points are introduced in an argument: According to van Fraassen, metaphysics as a discipline can be "shown up" by considering a single metaphysical question, e.g. whether the world exists (ES, p. 4). The ambitious reader should be enabled to "consider whether those flaws and failures do not also characterize more ambitious examples" (ES, p. 4).

1 Scientific Language

Let us take the challenge of leaving cosmology and take a closer look at point one to begin with. Van Fraassen argues:

> The metaphysical enterprise [...], subverts our understanding both of our own humanity and of the divine – be it real or unreal – by its development of a detailed, intricate understanding of simulacra under the same names. One example is the purport of discussing the God of Abraham, Isaac, and Jacob while actually focused on the God of the philosophers. But the same sort of replacement by theoretical simulacra characterizes the enterprise throughout. (ES, p. 4)

Facing the purported difficulty does not seem to be particularly complicated because the question does not arise for the first time. Carnap, for example, dedicates six pages of his "Logical Foundations of Probability" to "explication" in science.[3] He takes for granted that scientific language cannot cover all known implications of a prescientific term; thus he demands to sketch out this very term as clearly as possible, e.g. by giving examples. The result, a concept defined by means of every-day language, is called "explicandum". Its correspondent concept in science, the "explicatum", however is designed to fit into the target system of science and is defined by its special vocabulary.

3 Carnap (1950), pp. 3ff.

Next, Carnap formulates four criteria for an adequate explicatum: similarity to the explicandum, exactness, fruitfulness and simplicity. The interesting point is that these criteria may compete against each other. A strict demand for similarity may e.g. diminish fruitfulness critically. Concerning similarity an explicandum is succeeded by a satisfactory explicatum if the explicandum is no longer needed in scientific talk, but at the same time it is in most occasions still suitable for every-day language. Concerning fruitfulness a good explicatum fits well into the system of the science for which it is designed.

We admit that in philosophy we cannot operate with concepts occurring in every-day language. This shall not disturb us since we are well aware of its context-dependence. We can confine ourselves to concentrating on specific aspects of a given term which can be roughly sketched out. By doing that we create an explicandum. In using the term "world", for instance, philosophers can easily agree not to speak about "the earth" but rather about a totality.

Van Fraassen's critique goes further: he asks for the coincidence of a certain use of an every-day language term and its explicatum.[4] Our reply is – speaking with Carnap – that he overemphasizes the criterion of similarity. We want to argue that fruitfulness must finally be taken into consideration at this step of explication:

This can be illustrated by reference to the empirical sciences. They often give primacy to fruitfulness at the expense of similarity. Carnap exemplifies such a case depicting the differences between the prescientific concept of a fish (approximately: "animal living in the water") and the zoologist concept referred to by "fish". The latter turns out to be much more fruitful to science because "fish" according to the zoologist term have far more in common than animals living in the water. Similarity is still given as in most cases the explicandum and explicatum can be equally applied.

There is no doubt that *philosophical* argumentation can produce satisfying answers although philosophically explicated terms are used. Van Fraassen generously offers examples of terms which in our opinion require explication: "persons" and "conscious beings" are taken for granted, but metaphysical

4 ES, p. 19 [still referring to "world"]: "None of these [every-day language] uses are at all the distinctive philosophical use found in recent ontology [...]."

theories about them are rejected because they "purport to interpret what we already understand to be the case" (ES, p. 3). However, recent examples show that in borderline cases our pre-philosophical understanding of these terms does not suffice: Doctors e.g. are confronted with human beings in coma and wonder about their consciousness, jurists face patients suffering from senile dementia and have to decide when to deny them rights. In these cases, the decisions depend on the definition of "person". Thinking of problems arising in the field of bioethics the extrapolation of prescientific terminology beyond the bounds of every-day usage is absolutely crucial.

To summarize, we argue that fruitfulness should be considered when constructing explicata; the overemphasized demand for similarity should be reduced to a reasonable level. We are not handling simulacra as long as in most cases we can use the explicatum in every-day discourse as well. Considering fruitfulness we satisfy an – occasionally striking – demand for explanation which van Fraassen seems to overlook completely. In other words: because of a demand for explanation we accept that science occasionally complicates our use of language.

Returning to *cosmology* we acknowledge that things are more difficult. This convinces us that maybe a single question is not sufficient to "show up" the discipline of metaphysics. There are no common examples of a demand for explanation in the field of cosmology. The prescientific concept "world" may in many occasions guarantee successful communication. However, if cosmology can contribute to satisfy some kind of demand for explanation – directly or indirectly – we have to accept it (keeping in mind that van Fraassen admits that "we can hardly think of any philosophical subject without speaking of the world." (ES, p. 5)).

A further point: even if cosmology had no practical implication, every-day language would not necessarily fail to hold a concept which for example meets David Lewis's definition of a world: we argue that there is sufficient similarity with the broached OED headline "the universe or a region of it" (ES, p. 20). Although mostly "the universe" may denote a closed set, speakers of every-day language could occasionally mean a totality when speaking about "the world". In this case, the explicandum would almost completely coincide with its explicatum.

2 Experience and Metaphysics

Let us now turn to the second objection against metaphysics, its relation to experience. Even if we agree to treat *subjects of significance*, what van Fraassen seems to argue is that metaphysical *problems* do not emerge from experience but rather from mere logical thinking. Descartes' omniscient, omnipotent and omnibenevolent god e.g. is supposed to be a mental construction with the purpose of proving some of Descartes' metaphysical theses.[5] The problem of theodicy is supposed to appear afterwards when wondering if the construed theory of God succeeds "*in its own terms*" (ES, p. 29). Let us stop here and take a closer look at this argumentation: In our opinion, mainly experience – not logic – manifested the problem. Firstly, the concept of god was certainly not created by idle thinking without any intake of experience: Descartes tried to reconcile his *experience* of physical phenomena with the biblical concept of god, which he at least partly *experienced* by actually reading the bible. Secondly, pain and evil are clearly subjects of experience which seem to strikingly contradict God's benevolence. The question of how to reconcile the misfortune, harm and pain everybody can experience with our conception of God was discussed already in the bible (Hiob, letter to the Romans 9, 14).

It was experience, not just idle thinking, that created the problem; thus it cannot be a mere "children's puzzle" (ES, p. 29) without any significance.

Other examples immediately come to our mind: The theory that the suitability of laws of nature points to an intelligent Creator is quite obviously backed up by empirical examples of suitability – or at least apparent suitability. Finding unsuitable mechanisms in nature would prominently impair the plausibility of the physico-teleological argument cited by van Fraassen. Even though we admit that we need a concept of "suitability" or "pain and evil" when looking for it, *we cannot manage without experience.* Maybe the relation between design in nature and the existence of God is not as tight as some imagined, it still seems to be true that this argument relies on empirical evidence in a similar way as biological explanations of biological design.

5 ES, p. 1 (speaking of god): "He is of course omniscient, omnipotent, and omnibenevolent, and he is designed precisely so as to guarantee that that everything Descartes says is true."

The following is admittedly controversial: experience frequently enters metaphysics by another means: We think of thought experiments of the style Kant and Descartes conducted. Thought experiments such as Kant's thought-experiments on the left and right hand, as well as Descartes' method on doubt rely on experience in the following sense: the intuitions that play a prominent role in these thought-experiments are formed by prior experiences – as in some thought experiments by Galileo or Einstein. This leads us to qualify the statement that "there are no ontological experimentalists" (ES, p. 13).

All that shows that experience does contribute to metaphysical theories. A fall-back position would now be to admit the *intake* of experience in metaphysics but to argue that experience cannot be a criterion to *knock out* metaphysical positions, i.e. experience does not play a decisive role in metaphysical *theory choice* (cf. ES, p. 13).

One could argue that – by the physico-teleological argument – God cannot be conclusively verified, whereas in science viruses, for example, can be observed with an electron microscope. However, using an electron microscope is – according to van Fraassen – not a conclusive method to establish the existence of viruses (cf. CEN, p. 154). It seems that asking for conclusive verification by experience is asking too much both in the case of God and in the case of viruses.

The following analogy suggests itself: On the one hand a world showing suitable mechanisms, on the other symptoms of influenza, corresponding to the former an intelligent Creator, corresponding to the latter a DNA strand protected by proteins. The truth-makers are revelation in the first case and an electron microscope in the second. If it is allowed to accept a scientific theory about viruses, it should not be forbidden to consider a metaphysical theory about God.

Considering the presented analogy it must be emphasized that we have to strictly distinguish the question as to whether a theory can *in principle* be judged on experience from two arising problems in this specific case: a) the truth of the empirical data and b) the availability of these data / the ability to verify them. Doubting the data given by revelation would consequently not weaken the presented argumentation.

3 INFERENCE TO THE BEST EXPLANATION

At this stage van Fraassen's third objection could be presented: Inference to the best explanation is a risk-taking pursuit of truth. A theory which cannot be conclusively verified is only worth keeping if something of significance is at stake.

Quite obviously a not conclusively verified *scientific* theory, e.g. on a certain pathogen, has to be applied to treat the corresponding illness as its possible gain – helping numerous people – is considered significant. The risk of a treatment failure is to be considered of minor importance if in most cases the theory can be applied successfully.

What about *metaphysical* theories? According to van Fraassen:

> [In metaphysics] the gains to be contemplated are those of having true beliefs [...] and of being in a position to explain [...]. The risk is precisely that of acquiring false beliefs. The specter faced here is that we may end up having explained all that is dreamt of in our philosophies by intricately crafted postulates that are false [...]. So all there is to evaluate is the loss and gain of true beliefs *simpliciter*. (ES, pp. 15f.)

He illustrates this point by asking the question what we would regret more: humankind never having had access to Newton's physics which turned out to be false but made numerous mental and technical developments possible or never having had access to Descartes' dualism which – fortunately – did not survive long in its very form but was an important step in philosophy. By rejecting metaphysical developments van Fraassen seems to overlook that they made possible concepts he certainly would not want to miss. It seems quite plausible to us that Newtonian physics relies heavily on Descartes' metaphysics: His substance dualism was an important presupposition of Newton's physics. Before Descartes it was common to doubt that a mathematical description of nature captures its essence. Descartes argued that the essence of the corporeal world consists in what can be described in mathematical terms, rather than in substantial forms. This is Newton's starting point as the first sentence of the Principia makes clear.

Social achievements like human rights, democracy and an open society are not to be thought of without past metaphysics. Human rights for example are the result of a series of philosophical positions which at least were not completely non-metaphysical in van Fraassen's sense.

Furthermore the concepts "person" and "conscious being" are originated in the rejected metaphysics and as we have argued these metaphysical concepts are necessary for answering contemporary problems. Apparently even van Fraassen cannot manage without them: "I reject metaphysics, and still I'll say that you exist and that you are a person, a conscious being" (ES, p. 3). In our opinion rejecting metaphysics while still using these concepts would end up in a sort of schizophrenia: Buying traditional metaphysical concepts while claiming that they are part of idle discourse does not seem to result in a comfortable worldview at all.

Conclusion

According to van Fraassen, Metaphysics as we used to know it is finally dead. We, on the contrary, have tried to argue that there still seems to be a lot of life in this old dog yet. None of van Fraassen's arguments appeared to us as very compelling: He is surely right in pointing out that there is a gap between metaphysical terms and their everyday counterparts; but this is quite usual in scientific discourse and does not disqualify metaphysics as silly, senseless talk. He catches a certain truth in showing that the connection between metaphysical theses and experience is somewhat different than in the natural sciences; but this cannot weaken the view that most metaphysical arguments depend heavily on experience. And perhaps it is not as obvious as in the natural sciences that metaphysical theories have a certain practical value for the society; but we should not oversee that many social improvements in the last three centuries, though they may seem as self-evident to most of us, are hard-won achievements through philosophical (and metaphysical) discourse. Metaphysics has been declared to be dead for several times in human history; we have tried to assure that this was not for the last time.

REFERENCES

Carnap, Rudolf (1950): *Logical Foundations of Probability*. Chicago.

LAWS AND METAPHYSICS

Two burdens easily discarded?

Marius Backmann, Christian Suhm, Michael Trappe

Abstract: Bas van Fraassen is an avowed empiricist who dismisses a wide range of metaphysical notions. He clearly opposes most of today's analytic ontology. In particular, he does not believe in laws of nature. However, there seems to be a tension between his overall anti-metaphysical attitude and his thoroughgoing criticism of the notion of laws of nature. We will try to show that van Fraassen either has to accept some sort of modest metaphysics in order to uphold his dismissal of laws of nature, or to adopt a sceptical instead of negative standpoint towards laws of nature.

Keywords: laws of nature, necessity, metaphysics, skepticism

1 LAWS, NECESSITY, AND A DILEMMA

What are laws of nature? Obviously, laws of nature have close relationships to nature and to how nature 'actually' works. What happens in nature is usually seen as being determined by laws. Furthermore, it is agreed upon by most philosophers that laws of nature have to be generally true propositions that can be employed to describe facts and to explain processes. According to this view, it is a law of nature that two masses attract each other or that the amount of energy is conserved in natural processes.

However, laws of nature cannot simply be true universal statements. "No rivers past, present, or future, are rivers of Coca-Cola, or of milk." (LS, p. 27) is obviously not a law, despite the truth of the sentence quantifying over all rivers in the universe. Hence, there has to be more to a law of nature.

There must be special features in virtue of which some generally true sentences deserve to be counted as laws of nature. According to van Fraassen, these features can be accounted for by a cluster of at least five central criteria for lawlikeness a law of nature more or less has to fulfill (cf. LS, p. 38): universality, objectivity, relation to explanation and science, and, last but not least, necessity.

The crucial criterion, discussed most widely in the recent literature on laws of nature, is certainly necessity. Laws of nature, so many philosophers claim, state necessary relations between events, processes, universals or whatever other entities might be proposed as standing in the relevant relation. With necessity attached to the notion of laws it is possible, as van Fraassen points out, to draw the following inference: "*It is a law that A*", therefore "*It is necessary that A*" (LS, p. 39, italics by van Fraassen). However, in van Fraassen's view two serious problems emerge from the necessity criterion for laws of nature (cf. LS, p. 39):

a) Inference Problem: Can "A is true." be concluded from "It is a law that A."? If it is in virtue of A's necessity that this inference is valid the following problem arises.
b) Identification Problem: What gives a law A its necessity? Due to which property of the world are there necessary universally true propositions?

Van Fraassen believes that these two problems together pose a dilemma which is unsolvable for any account of laws. A solution to the first problem makes the second one impossible to solve and vice versa. In particular, van Fraassen demonstrates the 'mechanism' of the dilemma by explicitly examining the account of laws proposed by David Lewis, the necessitarian view on laws, and the universals account defended by David Armstrong (LS, ch. 3-5). In sum, he does not only draw the conclusion that currently there are no convincing accounts of laws available, but rather "that there are no laws of nature" (LS, p. 183) at all.

In a discussion on van Fraassen's *Laws and Symmetry* John Earman proposed a different account of laws, the so-called "M-R-L-account" (Mill-Ramsey-Lewis-account) according to which necessity is no criterion of laws and which, hence, circumvents van Fraassen's dilemma. In Earman's view, science aims at developing deductive systems (deductive closed sets of true sentences) whose basic theorems and axioms are candidates for laws of nature.[1]

However, since it might be the case that two or more systems are empirically equivalent, a question has to be posed. Which of these competing deductive systems gives us the laws of nature? Obviously, there have to be further criteria by which one of the rival systems can be marked out as the decisive one. Here, their simplicity and strength might be taken into account. But what does it mean for a deductive system to be simple and strong? Still a scenario in the history of science is conceivable in which two or more deductive systems fare equally well according to *different* standards of simplicity and strength.[2] An adherent of the M-R-L-account would like to exclude such a scenario, since it is fairly obvious that it leads to divergent assumptions as to what the laws of nature are or even to the claim that we have not yet found a law of nature at all. In view of this possibility Earman, following David Lewis, stresses that a closer look at the history of science shows that this never happened so far. If the development of science gives rise to the hope of finding a unique theoretical system that gives us a simple and strong description of nature, we should not hesitate to identify the axioms and theorems of this particular system with the laws of nature.

2 VAN FRAASSEN'S SKEPTICISM ABOUT LAWS

Van Fraassen's reaction to the above mentioned scenario of two or more competing deductive systems each providing candidates for laws of nature is very clear. If the adoption of the M-R-L-account renders possible long-lived and obstinate underdeterminations with respect to laws of nature, and if, in addition, it is presupposed that the aim of science is to reveal laws of nature, the account has to be abandoned altogether. According to van Fraassen, the success of science should not depend on lucky but contingent findings of unique and comprehensive deductive systems. Even in situations of vari-

1 Cf. Earman (1993), p. 416.

2 This scenario and possible reactions to it are discussed in Earman (1993), pp. 417f.

ous but mutually incompatible axiomatized theories which equally well fit to a certain domain of phenomena science is to be counted among men's fruitful and worthwhile activities. If it comes to the question of adequacy to scientific practice of a proposed reconstruction of science, it is the demand for laws of nature that has to go. Although van Fraassen is quite sympathetic with Earman's critique of necessitarian views of laws and his pleading for seriously taking scientific practice into account, he is skeptical about the prospects of any approach whatsoever which gives laws center stage in the reconstruction of scientific activities.

On closer inspection van Fraassen's thorough dismissal of laws of nature in general, and his refusal of the M-R-L-account defended by Earman in particular, gives rise to at least two overall epistemological options. Both of them show some plausibility in the light of van Fraassen's recent empiricist and anti-metaphysical considerations.

According to the first option, one is still justified to believe in laws of nature although their truth and applicability is restricted to certain theoretical background assumptions. On this reading, what is called a law of nature is bound to the axioms and theorems of a deductive system or, to echo Kuhn, to a scientific paradigm. The concept of a scientific paradigm usually comprises scientific communities' basic ontological commitments, central scientific notions and methodologies, strategies for solving so-called scientific puzzles and so on.[3] Laws of nature would no longer be conceived of as fundamental principles of nature being absolutely independent of our theories and concepts, but rather as being man-made in the sense of being relative to a particular scientific paradigm. As one can easily see this option comes close to some sort of constructivism which, roughly, makes the structure of reality, especially its nomological texture, a matter of scientific perspective.

Much of what van Fraassen recently claimed with regard to the question of theory-dependence of any structure we ascribe to reality also seems to favor a constructivist interpretation of laws (cf. LE). As he frankly advocates, the structure of reality we assume in scientific theories should be regarded as deeply theory- or language-dependent. Consequently, he considers the idea of

3 Cf. Kuhn (1970), especially section 2 (pp. 181-187) of the postscript Kuhn added to the second edition of *The Structure of Scientific Revolutions*.

a theory-independent structure of reality to be detected or revealed by science as radically fallacious. (Cf. LE, pp. 351ff.)

But we should be cautious here with hasty conclusions. As far as we see, van Fraassen nowhere explicitly claims that laws are to be conceived of as something we impose on nature by adopting a particular scientific paradigm. On the contrary, he restricts the role of laws to 'verbalizing' necessary relations between elements of models, rather than elements of reality. Therefore, it seems to be more in line with van Fraassen's overall model-theoretic conception of theories and laws to pursue a skeptical reading of laws.

According to this second epistemological option our attitude towards laws should be agnostic. Since laws are, at best, necessary relations between elements of *models* which we usually cannot observationally confirm to be necessary relations between elements *of reality* as well, we are in no way entitled to believe in any nomological structure of reality. This line of reasoning seems to be much more in line with van Fraassen's reactions to various conceptions of laws of nature, and especially accords with his response to Earman's defense of the M-R-L-account. Van Fraassen concludes that if laws are to be identified with axioms or theorems appearing in each optimal deductive system – optimal with respect to simplicity and strength –, and if it is the aim of science to find such laws, then it might turn out by contingent historical reasons that scientific activity is completely on the wrong track. But since it appears highly implausible to hinge the odds of science upon the contingencies of its branched history, van Fraassen is able to readily counter Earman's approach to laws by a rhetorical question:

> Imagine those unlikely conditions obtain, and science is definitely not on the road to delivering to us the laws of this world [...] Under that supposition, wouldn't you still say that the science we have is a worthwhile and very successful enterprise, and not a failure? (PLS, p. 434)

If we understand van Fraassen's critique of Earman's account of laws of nature (and that of many others) correctly, his main concern is centered upon the criterion of adequacy to scientific practice. Hence, any concept of law which is at variance with what scientific activity aims at and which lends no credence to the success of science falls short of that criterion. It is only laws of models which, according to van Fraassen, pass the test of adequacy to science.

Obviously, van Fraassen's thoroughgoing doubts about finding an adequate concept of law of nature motivate his anti-realist attitude towards nomological structures of the physical reality. However, one might ask whether he is justified in advocating "the philosophical view that there are no laws of nature" (LS, p. 183). Is it not once more a *skeptical* conclusion that is licensed by van Fraassen's critical analyses of extant accounts of laws, rather than an *ontological* one as to the non-existence of laws of nature? To our minds, it is one thing to be skeptical or agnostic about the nomological make-up of nature, and another one to outright neglect it. So if van Fraassen really wants to make us believe that any concept of law of nature is totally misguided, further investigations into the metaphysical consequences of the concept of law seem to be inevitable. Here one seriously wonders whether this is the road the avowed anti-metaphysician van Fraassen is willing to take. In the final section of our paper we will elaborate on this question.

3 About Becoming a Metaphysician When You Do Not Want To

So what does van Fraassen do as the kind of empiricist he describes himself? Firstly, he insists on the criterion of necessity for "any acceptable account of laws" (LS, pp. 38f.) which is part of his cluster-account of laws. (LS, p. 28) And secondly, since he demonstrated that this criterion cannot be fulfilled, he explicitly denies the very existence of laws in contrast to eschewing the notion of a law. (Cf. LS, pp. 183, 214)

In this he disagrees with his fellow empiricist Norman Swartz. In his works which will in part be discussed below Swartz portrays himself as a good epistemological skeptic and admits that we have, in particular, no epistemological access to laws of nature. What Swartz does indeed is to accept questions of the nomological structure of reality as metaphysical ones.[4] We will discuss now why he does so and will follow him in this regard.

4 Cf. Swartz (1995), p. 73.

Although Swartz is an adherent of the regularity theory of causality, he maintains that – critical analysis assured – one cannot avoid making metaphysical statements, be they positive or negative, in the reconstruction of science. This accepted it becomes questionable whether it is possible to give an adequate reconstruction of scientific practice without considering at least such basic metaphysical notions as causality or laws of nature.[5] Swartz, indeed, has a very wide notion of metaphysics. But in our view he, as a regularity theorist, is right to do so, as everything that goes beyond regular experiences falls within the realm of metaphysics. One should note that Swartz's concept of laws of nature explicitly excludes necessity and that he does not believe in nomicity in nature.[6] This, according to Swartz himself, already counts as a metaphysical consideration.[7]

Moreover, often metaphysical questions stand at the very beginning of scientific scrutiny although they cannot be solved by the sciences at all. That there is/is not something like a free will is and always will be a metaphysical question, as it, e.g., heavily depends on whether there is a correlation of mental processes to neural ones and whether there is some sort of determination of the former by the latter, or vice versa. Whether one is a physicalist might also be important for that question. But the debate on free will inspired scientists like Eccles, Libet, Roth and Singer to do a lot of neurological research.[8] As science relies upon metaphysical concepts[9] and its practice is guided by them, it is highly questionable whether van Fraassen's empirical stance that is explicitly anti-metaphysical can be adequate to scientific practice. It is, however, more than obvious that the demand for adequacy to science is central to van Fraassen's overall empiricist leanings. (Cf. ES, p. 55)

5 Cf. ibid., p. 75; Swartz (2001), p. 42.
6 Cf. ibid., p. 71.
7 Since on his account the notion of law does not include necessity, he avoids the above mentioned dilemma of inference and identification.
8 Indeed it seems that much of this neurological research would be pointless without the aforementioned metaphysical debate about free will, as some of the conclusions drawn from neurological results are deeply metaphysical and the aim of such inquiry often is to prove metaphysical statements. Much research has been done to show that there is no free will, which by any means is a metaphysical statement.
9 Cf. Swartz (2001), pp. 41f.

Swartz's understanding of metaphysics and its role in science is nothing like the kind of ambitious analytic ontology or 17th century-like metaphysics van Fraassen attacks in *The Empirical Stance*. In science, by pursuing metaphysical concerns, there is more to be won than just presenting at best "coherent nonsense" (ES, p. 17), since metaphysical concepts, the concept of laws of nature in particular, have at least some theoretical as well as practical relevance. To accept them seems to be a quite modest form of metaphysics in contrast to recent forms of analytic ontology and highly speculative 17th century and idealist metaphysics. The latter ones are accused by Fraassen of perverting well understood common sense concepts, as for example the concept of world, "into something hardly anyone understands" (ES, p. 5).

At this point one must not assume that the whole lot of ambitious but fruitless metaphysics enters theorizing about laws again. Swartz favors "scientific laws" instead of laws of nature, calling the latter ones philosophical "arcana"[10]. He construes scientific laws as being completely man-made. According to him, strictly speaking all of them are known to be false and extremely idealized.[11] Since Swartz rejects a necessitarian account of laws of nature, there is no need to view scientific theorizing about physical laws as an activity that includes any kind of metaphysical consideration.

Van Fraassen on the other hand denies being trapped within metaphysics as he radically denies the existence of something as metaphysically loaded as laws of nature. (Cf. LS, p. 183)[12] But is van Fraassen a good empiricist in doing so? According to his reconstruction of David Hume, Swartz states that a real Humean – as she is recently understood e.g. by Galen Strawson and John

10 An arcanum is understood here as a mystic, occult and secret power or knowledge of such a hidden power.

11 Cf. Swartz (1995), p. 72. The notion of necessity, by the way, would be unproblematic in this account, as it would be merely verbal. There could be no inferences to anything outside the scientific discourse.

12 In *The Empirical Stance* van Fraassen makes the very same move with regard to the existence of God. As he does not want to engage in metaphysics, he is convinced that there is no God. By any means he should refrain from this conviction if he really wants not to pursue any metaphysical considerations. (ES, p. 3) To say that it is the God of the metaphysicians that does not exist does not help in this regard, as a common sense concept of God (if there is any) is not less metaphysical as a metaphysician's. The latter one is just more explicitly so.

P. Wright[13] – must remain an epistemological skeptic about such things as laws or other metaphysical entities. This sort of skepticism does not involve statements of non-existence but rather implies an epistemic reserve, which is paralleled by the pyrrhonic skeptic's virtue of epochē.

Van Fraassen does a very different thing. As we have already mentioned, he explicitly says that there are no laws of nature (Cf. LS, p. 183), which is a negative statement of existence no epistemological skeptic in a pyrrhonic tradition could maintain. This negative statement is indeed as metaphysical as the opposed positive one. So if van Fraassen really wants to avoid any metaphysical statements, for example statements of analytic ontology, he should perhaps be more of a real Humean, i.e. a more humble skeptic adopting the attitude of epochē with regard to statements about the existence or non-existence of metaphysical entities.

It seems that van Fraassen drives into a dilemma here. *Either* he insists on eschewing metaphysics – be they modest or ambitious – and gives up his radical rejection of laws of nature. *Or* he accepts a sort of modest metaphysics in his reconstruction of scientific reasoning and will thereby still be able to avoid at least ambitious metaphysics with respect to laws of nature. If he accepts modest metaphysics his empiricism, allegedly anti-metaphysical, would be founded upon metaphysical considerations. This may not lead to undesirable consequences as long as it is only critical analysis of metaphysical questions that is needed but no metaphysical 'excess' like necessitarianism.

To sum up: we believe that there is a curious tension in van Fraassen's empiricism between being anti-metaphysical on the one hand, and making metaphysical statements on the other. This tension could be released by accepting modest metaphysical considerations and by avoiding metaphysical 'excesses'. From this it follows that van Fraassen's approach to laws needs serious adjustment either if he wants to be a good anti-metaphysical empiricist or if he accepts modest metaphysics. In the first case he could discard metaphysics, but then he would be unable to outright reject laws of nature. In the second case he would have to engage in metaphysics or analytic ontology and by that might be entitled to claim that there are no laws of nature. He can only discard either metaphysics or laws of nature which both seem to burden

13 Cf. Swartz 1995, p. 82.

him. Discarding both of them is not as easy as van Fraassen wants to make us believe.

REFERENCES

Earman, John (1993): "In Defense of Laws: Reflections on Bas van Fraassen's *Laws and Symmetry*", *Philosophy and Phenomenological Research* LIII, pp. 413-419.

Kuhn, Thomas S. (1970): *The Structure of Scientific Revolutions*. Chicago: University of Chicago Press.

Swartz, Norman (1995): „A Neo-Humean Perspective: Laws as Regularities", in Friedel Weinert (ed.): *Laws of Nature. Essays on the Philosophical, Scientific and Historical Dimensions*. Berlin and New York: Walter de Gruyter, pp. 67-91.

Swartz, Norman (2001): *Beyond Experience. Metaphysical Theories and Philosophical Constraints*. 2nd edition. Toronto: Toronto University Press.

EMPIRICISM WITHOUT METAPHYSICS?

On van Fraassen's conception of a stance[1]

Sebastian Muders

Abstract: In this paper I try to demonstrate that van Fraassen's own conception of empiricism as a stance is deeply infected with something he has tried to leave far behind in what he calls naïve empiricism – namely fundamental beliefs. Van Fraassen's stance empiricism together with the introduction of values, attitudes and commitments as its essential parts cannot free empiricism from fundamental beliefs – at least insofar as only these beliefs can justify the mentioned elements of a stance here, and at least insofar as stance empiricism should be as discussable as his naïve predecessor. In the end, van Fraassen's conception of stance empiricism gives us the picture of a kind of empiricism which does not consist solely in beliefs but nevertheless totally depends upon them.

Keywords: empiricism, stance

INTRODUCTION

Van Fraassen not only argues against recent metaphysics as an important segment of philosophical thinking, but he also tries to go a step further: What could philosophy be beyond the metaphysical projects, expressed in ontological problems like the existence of god or the world? – Not surprisingly, van Fraassen insists that empiricism generally goes in the right direction and is, after the death of metaphysics, its legitimate successor in Philosophy. But "empiricism" is at first a mere four-syllable expression – what exactly is it,

1 I would like to express my deep gratefulness to Andreas Hüttemann, who helped me with several discussions to write this paper and has given me many helpful comments and proposals to refine it.

what theses does it hold, and is it really beyond or at least free from all metaphysical burden? – To answer these questions accurately, we first need to know what van Fraassen exactly means when he uses the word "metaphysics"; we need to know the *corpus delicti* of metaphysical thinking in order to find out what van Fraassen's own position is in this debate. For I have the suspicion that van Fraassen indeed denies all metaphysical speculation on the one hand, but tries to smuggle an important characteristic of this kind of philosophy into his own theory on the other. More precisely, I believe that van Fraassen tries to create a philosophical position which we would call an "eierlegende Wollmilchsau" in German – a perfect all-in-one-solution suitable for nearly every purpose – only with the little flaw that it has a contradiction in itself. Van Fraassen tries to capture two irreconcilable principles: On one side his position should not consist solely in beliefs, such as naïve empiricism does; on the other, it should offer a sufficient basis for rational discourse about it. The dilemma I see is this: Rational discourse is only possible as far as the elements of a stance rest ultimately on beliefs or some other equivalent truth-bearing entities; so we conclude that either there is a deep dependence between these other elements and the beliefs, which would be the status of naïve empiricism: You can only hold any part of the stance if you hold the beliefs which generate it, so there is no real development compared to the case of naïve empiricism. Or you try to solve the connection between beliefs and non-beliefs, on pain of loosing the possibility to argue rationally about the elements under consideration.

1 Van Fraassen's conception of a stance

The problem: Empiricism's self-defeating argument against metaphysics

When van Fraassen describes the traditional understanding of empiricism which he calls naïve empiricism, he presents us a powerful argument which empiricism can indeed use against all variants of dogmatism, i.e. not empirically proceeding metaphysics, but only with the devastating consequence of its own demolition (cf. ES, pp. 41-45):

(1) All philosophical positions consist in one fundamental thesis X which makes certain assertions about the world.
(2) In the case of empiricism, this thesis X could be specified as "Experience is the one and only source of information." – Let this thesis be the *conditio sine qua non* for empiricism.
(3) Each kind of empiricism also admires the (natural) sciences and adopts some of their methodological assumptions, for instance that disagreement with any admissible factual hypothesis is itself admissible.
(4) So empiricism cannot hold any thesis dogmatically without justifying it on the tribunal of experience.
(5) The fundamental thesis of empiricism is in itself not falsifiable against any experience and therefore not justified.
(6) Thus this thesis is not tenable for empiricism.

(C) Empiricism is wrong.

The solution: Empiricism as a stance

To avoid this devastating conclusion and save empiricism, van Fraassen offers us his conception of a stance: In brief, philosophical positions, re-interpreted as a stance, are not systematic structures of beliefs anymore, which together form a specific picture about the world; instead, they are interpreted as a collection "[that] consist[s] in something other than [...] belief[s] in what the world is like". More precisely, they consist in "attitudes, commitments, values, goals, [...] a cluster of such – possibly including some propositional attitudes such as beliefs as well." (ES, pp. 47f.) We notice that beliefs *qua* beliefs are not a great problem for a stance, only if they take a certain position inside it – namely, a fundamental position, if they are used to justify other elements of the stance. For then the argument goes the same destructive way for stance empiricism as it went for metaphysics and naïve empiricism: If the final justification of my philosophical position consists in beliefs, then we have a result which van Fraassen himself cannot accept: We have to stick to these beliefs dogmatically, for they are *per definitionem* the very last source in your epistemology, and since the whole stance depends on them, there would be no practical difference between this kind of philosophical position and naïve empiricism. It follows that the other elements of the stance must have a somewhat different nature. – The great advantage van Fraassen sees in these elements is their truth-less nature: The fact that they cannot be distinguished as true or false propositions makes them of course less attractive for scientific study:

> If empiricism is a stance, its critique of metaphysics will be based at least in part on something other than factual theses [...]. Now it is quite clear in the example of empirical science that disagreement in that sphere does not stay within the scientific family. (ES, p. 48)

Let us take a closer look at the other possible candidates of a stance: At least in the case of attitudes, it seems rather clear that they cannot serve as good examples of possible truth- or falsehood: If I am angry with my neighbor, for instance, for playing his music too loud, I take a negative attitude towards him. But given that I am in fact angry, nobody can declare my anger to be false in any propositional way. Instead, someone can judge it as inappropriate or to be expressing the right behavior in the present situation – but these are normative judgments, and they are rarely found in descriptive natural or social sciences, which van Fraassen may have primarily in mind when he speaks about the "scientific family". The second mentioned candidate here, values, seems to be a more tricky case, but we grant van Fraassen, that these possible elements in his stance are free of any truth- or falsehood.

2 TWO ACCOUNTS OF POSSIBLE DISCOURSE BESIDES TRUTH- AND FALSEHOOD

Van Fraassen maintains that you can interpret nearly every philosophical position in the light of his stance-conception; we want to emphasize that in our opinion, he has given a well described and fruitful conception about philosophical positions in general and empiricism in particular. But nevertheless, his solution raises a new interesting question: If even metaphysics does not have a believe-founded fundament anymore, then surely his argument concerning metaphysics would not work properly? But then, how is one supposed to decide between different, mutually excluding philosophical theories as stances? Van Fraassen seems to have two different replies to this challenge.

Consistency and a common ground

You can find the first answer in his reply to a paper presented at the Symposium of the American Philosophical Association in 2004. Here he picks up a picture of his stance-conception given by Anjan Chakravartty: According to this picture, a philosophical position consists of three different parts: At the top we see several beliefs, one step below we have the corresponding epistemic stances which generate these beliefs and at the bottom we finally find so-called stances in epistemology (cf. van Fraassen (2004), pp. 11f.). The differences between these two forms of stances are of no importance to us here. Since van Fraassen recognizes that the introduction of new levels inside a stance only shifts the question of how to proceed and decide between competing stances, he argues that we can rationally choose among rival stances first in terms of their consistency. But we believe that this does not help us much here: For it is plausible to argue that more than enough mutually excluding stances will remain, even if we apply the consistency-criterion to them. So van Fraassen is in need to bring another criterion into the discourse: He maintains that we could argue on the basis of common values which we share even among otherwise different stances. But then the differences between the stances are either not existent and both opponents simply speak a different language, or one of them makes a mistake and has therefore one or more false beliefs – a result not tenable for van Fraassen, as we saw above. Or the differences are indeed too deep to solve them on the basis of rational arguments – but then the problem does not vanish, and we might ask once more: How to proceed, how to decide? – At last here van Fraassen's argumentation becomes a little difficult to understand: He maintains that someone can acknowledge someone else's values without leaving his own ground (cf. van Fraassen (2004), p. 11). But what would be the improvement in a discussion if I accept someone else's attitudes, beliefs or values, but nevertheless think that mine are the right ones? At best, we then have an exchange of incompatible views and do not understand the other's motivations nor could convince him in one or the other way – because every conviction must be based on shared beliefs, and here no shared beliefs exist *ex hypothesi.* To put it in other words, it seems that we have reached something we can name stance-relativism – a result which cannot satisfy van Fraassen's original intentions, for as we have seen in "There is life in the old dog yet!", he thinks that we can argue in favor of empiricism and against metaphysical thinking through rational argumentation.

Normative dimensions besides Truth- and Falsehood

The second answer he gives seems to us more promising: He claims that there could be disagreement and rational discourse even outside the sphere of true or false beliefs and writes:

> Now it is quite clear in the example of empirical science that disagreement in that sphere does not stay within the scientific family. A disregard for evidence, a refusal to submit one's ideas to natural selection by relevant experiment or to engage in vigorous testing when nature itself does not put one to the test (these are some examples, none of them factual beliefs!) can certainly take one beyond the scientific pale. So the paradigm of science does not suggest that disagreement in the sphere of attitudes, commitments, values and goals is invulnerable to empiricist critique. (ES, p. 48)

What form of disagreement could van Fraassen have in mind here? – As we have already sketched above, the closest answer to this is probably the introduction of new normative dimensions like appropriateness in the case of attitudes or usefulness in the case of commitments. This move has the advantage that we need not speak of truth or falsehood anymore but can nevertheless insist that we can have a rational discussion about the virtues and flaws of philosophical positions. This argument sounds good – but it has the decisive premise that our arguments in favor of or against the appropriateness of an attitude or a commitment does not depend on true beliefs about the way the world is – for if this were the case, our commitments are founded on such beliefs, and this would be a consequence which van Fraassen could hardly accept: Stance empiricism would then run into the same difficulties as naïve empiricism.

3 THE TRUTH-DEPENDENCE OF PHILOSOPHICAL STANCES

Stances as policies

Let us have a closer look at the nature of a stance: In his review of van Fraassen's ES, Paul Teller asks "What is a stance?" and tries to elaborate a functional characterization of this kind of entity. He generates a fruitful analogy to which we and van Fraassen give our applause[2], namely an analogy between stances and policies: In his view, stances are "guidelines for ways to form and evaluate beliefs"[3] and are insofar similar to "adopting a policy"[4]; because to adopt a policy is "to resolve or to commit oneself to acting or making decisions as described by the statement of the policy".[5] And this, at least that is van Fraassen's proposal, is the way we should also interpret philosophical stances: As guidelines for our epistemic behavior and judgments. And echoing van Fraassen, Teller insists that a stance is "not something that is true or false. Instead policies are evaluated as being well or ill advised, conducive to certain ends, easy or difficult to administer, and in many other practical respects." – Up to this point, Teller has our unrestricted consent; but we go on and ask the question: We grant that a policy is not in itself something which can be true or false; *but what about the reasons for adopting a policy?* And what kind of entities could these "reasons" be? We are going to show that they are nothing else but beliefs; and if all elements of a stance depend on foregoing beliefs, what about van Fraassen's attempt to leave behind fundamentalism as a wrong-guided epistemological position in metaphysics or naïve empiricism? –

2 Compare for instance van Fraassen's dictum in his reply on Teller: "Teller explores the idea that a stance may be more or less the same as a policy, and Lipton too takes this up. This provides valuable insight into the concept." (RDES, p. 174)

3 Teller (2004), p. 163.

4 Ibid., p. 166.

5 Ibid.

To answer these questions, we have to take a closer look at these elements which can take part in a philosophical stance besides the beliefs.

Attitudes

To make a fresh start, Teller himself emphasizes that a policy depends at least in part on beliefs, especially in the case of attitudes. He gives us the following example: "I might have a policy never to wear brown because I am slightly blue/green colorblind and so have difficulty judging which browns match."[6] Here my belief that I am colorblind functions evidently as a reason for my negative attitude against brown clothes. And if I found out that I had simply been wrong to hold that assumption, then there would be *ceteris paribus* no longer a good reason for me not to wear brown clothes. But, one might ask, are there not at least some attitudes which do not depend on foregoing beliefs? Well, we can hardly imagine which sort of attitudes would fit this description, for even such comparatively basic attitudes as my anger about my neighbor's loud music is well founded in my belief that it is my neighbor who is responsible for that music; and if it turned out that he does not even own a radio, then I would have no reason to be angry with him anymore. More to the point, van Fraassen's own scanty examples of attitudes which found entry in the empirical stance exhibit a great deal more complexity – that is, complexity with respect to the beliefs involved: The admiration for natural sciences as one of these attitudes which appeared in the empirical stance depends, for instance, to a very high extent on beliefs: It rests on the assumption that sciences are successful in their description and explanation of natural phenomena, that the scientific research of the 19th and 20th century gives us a great variety of positive examples for this, and so on.[7]

6 Teller (2004), p. 166.

7 An analogous point could be made if we take a closer look at van Fraassen's own example of a metaphysical stance, namely materialism: If we try to characterize materialism as an attitude which can remain unchanged even if the physical sciences develop and construe new, at first glimpse "immaterial" entities to get an adequate theory about the world, the main reason for this would be that the theses which underlie these attitudes are rather rough – and even here there are obvious constraints: The positive attitude materialism forms towards the physical sciences, that "science

Values

A similar point could be made when we come to the next significant element in a stance: values. Again, Teller demonstrates their importance by stressing once more the analogy between stances and policies: "Policies are, sometimes explicitly, sometimes implicitly, expressions or implementations of values. To adopt the policy of not lying is an explicit expression of values."[8] When we check our intuitions and ask ourselves how we would justify our moral policy not to lie, would it be a good answer to refer, with an indefinite shrugging, to a feeling in our stomach? – Surely a better way to deal with the problem would be to cite some of our moral or non-moral beliefs which at least implicitly postulate to catch a correct picture of the world: That you should not lie, since you not only betray the people who trust you but you also damage your reputation; that it is much more difficult to cover a lie with other lies than simply speak truthfully and so on.

We agree that the nature of normative judgments is anything but a trivial case. And perhaps many philosophers would argue that the examples of the beliefs given above are not very persuasive, for they appear to them to be a little elliptic: According to them, a more full-blooded version of the first belief is "You should not lie, since you betray the people who trust you – *and that's wrong*." Without this addendum, the belief in itself could not count as a sufficient reason for the negative value I give to the act of lying. On the other hand, it has no descriptive end but functions only as an expression of my own feelings, therefore, like in the case of attitudes, we cannot discuss them.

But this counter-objection can be met in several ways: First, van Fraassen declares that he does not want to put forward an over-simplified version of a value-theory: He speaks about the improvements philosophy has gained since the days of Ayer's "Truth, Language and Logic" and adds: "[We know well] how to defeat the simplistic philosophies that make values just a matter of subjective preference, dismissably relative." (ES, p. 62) So we can conclude

teaches us what to believe" (ES, p. 63) is in need for a justification in terms of beliefs.

8 Teller (2004), p. 167.

that he is at least no friend of any subjective account of values. Furthermore, van Fraassen allows rational discourse even in the field of values:

> We [...] are members of a highly politicized open society in which ethical and ideological differences are precisely what ate most up for debate. We need not look far to see that rational discourse is possible on matters that touch our values, attitudes, and commitments. (ES, p. 62)

So let us agree that we indeed have long disputes on questions about values, at least in democratic societies like our own. Consider the example of abortion: Here both sides argue by means of arguments which of course includes values like the right of the fetus to life, or the right of the woman to decide for herself; but they do so with the expectation that we can, at least in principle, handle all these value-statements like facts, that we can use them to persuade the other side analogous to other, purely descriptive disputes. They try to give their reasons a basis in reality even if they refer to more general values the other side possesses in order to derivate the importance of the values they defend out of them. Because both the postulate that both sides share similar values as well as the derivation of some values out of others are factual theses, theses about the world, and thus both sides are in need to establish such truth-loaded entities to find a beginning in their conversation. So van Fraassen is confronted with the decision between either conceding that our values stand on the ground of beliefs and are therefore discussable or rejecting this view on the loss of meaningful discourse about the questionable values under consideration.

4 TWO FINAL OBJECTIONS

One belief or many?

There is no need to examine a further candidate, the commitments: The argument will come to very much the same conclusions. In this final section, we would like to respond to two possible arguments against our hitherto sketched position: First, one could argue that so far we have only shown that even stance empiricism rests on beliefs – but that was not van Fraassen's main point in this debate: His argument was not that naïve empiricism is founded on several beliefs, *but that it depends on only one belief*, so that the empiricist cannot allow any doubts about it without irreversibly undermining his own position. But in our case, the stance empiricist has many beliefs available and thus need not make any dogmatic assertions about any of them. So does our argument simply miss the point after all? – Well, this would only be the case if van Fraassen concedes that naïve empiricism is all right as soon as it can give us a second, not further derivable principle – and he may have good reasons not to allow this: For then all the values, commitments and attitudes as the essential characteristics of a stance would become superfluous at once! More to the point, the naïve empiricist can use a simple trick to reach this comfortable position against stance empiricism: He only has to split up his basic belief "Experience is the one and only source of information" into many different, for example: "What someone sees is one important source of information" plus "What someone hears is one important source of information" and so on. Furthermore, we can sum up all the individual beliefs in van Fraassen's stance into one great belief if we simply use the conjunction to bring them together. And finally, van Fraassen's conception as a whole rests ultimately on the belief that his stance-conception is an adequate picture for philosophical positions, or at least for empiricism – and therefore subject to the same objections than naïve empiricism.

Teller or van Fraassen?

The second possible objection may be that our attempt to give an adequate interpretation of the stance-conception has failed because we refer to the wrong source: Too much Teller, too little van Fraassen, so to speak. But if we take a closer look at the few hints and examples van Fraassen gives us in ES[9], we find other analogies which seem to contain a strong similarity to Teller's suggestion: To adopt a stance is for van Fraassen "similar or analogous to conversion to a cause, a religion, an ideology, to capitalism or socialism [...]

9 For the empiricist stance, see ES, pp. 47f., for a metaphysical one see ES, pp. 58-63.

[or] to a worldview." (ES, p. 61) All these examples surprise us insofar as they would be our own ones, if we were asked to mention some examples of a good belief-based policy: When I adopt a religion, an ideology or some other kind of worldview, I do so because I am strongly convinced of their goals, their diagnosis they give about the world or the truth of the epiphany in their holy books. In either case, I have various beliefs which justify my adopting them, and if these beliefs were wrong, I would have no rational reason to hold them any longer.

Conclusion

Let us summarize: I have tried to demonstrate that van Fraassen's own conception of a stance is deeply infected with something he has tried to leave far behind in naïve empiricism – namely the fundamental beliefs. He asks: "Suppose that empiricism is a stance rather than a thesis; how does that get empiricism out of trouble?" (ES, p. 48) My answer is simple: It doesn't get empiricism out of trouble, since even van Fraassen's own stance empiricism together with the introduction of values, attitudes and commitments as its essential parts cannot free empiricism from its fundamental beliefs – at least insofar as only these beliefs can justify the mentioned elements of a stance here, and at least insofar as stance empiricism should be as discussable as his naïve predecessor. Finally, van Fraassen's conception of stance empiricism gives us the picture of a kind of empiricism which does not consist solely in beliefs but nevertheless totally depends upon them, at least if empiricism should not be a mere expression of our feelings but a discussable subject in philosophical-scientific discourse.

References

van Fraassen, Bas C. (2004): Reply to Chakravartty, Jauernig, and McMullin, APA Pasadena, March 2004, text available on the author's website: http://www.princeton.edu/~fraassen/abstract/ReplyAPA-04.pdf

Teller, Paul (2004): "Discussion – What is a Stance?", *Philosophical Studies* 121, pp. 159-170.

REPLIES TO THE PAPERS

Bas C. van Fraassen

Participation in the *Münstersche Vorlesungen zur Philosophie 2005* was an honor and a genuine intellectual pleasure for me. The symposium, with all its contributions by the Münster faculty and students, was a wonderfully valuable experience. I can hardly do justice to its spirit of free discussion, or adequately express my thanks, by these short replies. But I think that they will testify clearly to the stimulation the symposium provided and to how much I learned from this exchange.

PREAMBLE: ON LITERATE EXPERIENCE AND REALISM

It was a special pleasure for me to see the attention paid in several papers to my "Literate Experience: the [De-, Re-] Interpretation of Nature". I was concerned there with certain parallels I saw between literary theory and philosophy of science. Because of its context, I allowed myself to write it in a rather literary style, and enjoyed the exercise. But a literary style lends itself perhaps more easily to construal and misconstrual. Before responding to the individual papers, therefore, I will do something to make its main ideas somewhat clearer.

We can begin with a point about experience in *The Scientific Image.* There is a difference between *observation* and *observation that* – that is to say, between observing something and observing that it is thus or so. We make this distinction easily for seeing and hearing: I saw the yellow candy wrapper in the grass but took it to be a flower, I heard the Lorelei's song but did not hear that it was the Lorelei's song, I took it for the sound of the Rhine's waves on the shore.

Experience has two faces. On the one hand it is simply what happens to us, of which we are aware. On the other hand it is the content of the spontaneous judgement in response to what happens. What happened was that I saw the yellow candy wrapper. My spontaneous judgement was that I was seeing a flower. A simple mistake, which highlights the distinction between the two sides of the experience. Of course I usually make no such mistakes. But a distance between the two sides can be discerned in more serious ways.

> Suppose one of the Stone Age people recently found in the Philippines is shown a tennis ball or a car crash. From his behaviour, we see that he has noticed them; for example, he picks up the ball and throws it. But he has not seen *that* it is a tennis ball, or *that* some event is a car crash, for he does not even have those concepts. (SI, p. 15)

The spontaneous judgements we can make are ones that we can express in the language we have. This language may lack certain resources, and this limits the second side of our experience, although what can happen to us is the same as what can happen to anyone at all. On the other hand our language may be in a certain sense too rich, because it is theory-laden, and the theory that has helped to shape it adds implications that go far beyond the immediate deliverances of experience. I fall over something and judge it to be a radio. Suppose that the concept of *radio*, the sense of my word "radio", is such that nothing can instantiate it unless there are electromagnetic waves. Then my spontaneous judgement in response to what happened implies that there are electromagnetic waves, though that was quite possibly more than was needed to express what I knew. Later on we may say that it was too much – as we would now say of cries of "Phlogiston escaping!" in response to fire. Once again we can highlight the distance clearly only by attention to cases where we (the current speakers and hearers) see a mismatch.

Notice how my discussion of all this has been realistic throughout. Nothing in what I said implied that there is no matter of fact about what happens to us, nor that we are unable to find out what did happen.[1] But being realistic does not mean being either a scientific or metaphysical realist. In fact it is those realists who may tend to suspect that this way of describing our situation is a road to philosophical ruin, that it will lead us into a debilitating skepticism or subjective idealism.

What nature is like does not depend on what our experience or representation of nature is like. *But we must not confuse this point with a naive realism about how we ourselves exist in this world.* As for us, we discern structure in nature; but the structure we discern there, we discern in the same way as we discern a story when looking at ink marks on a page. (cf. LE, p. 354)

The spontaneous judgements we make in response to what happens to us are ones expressible in the language we have at the time – they are readings of the events in question. The fact that nature is not created thereby becomes manifest to us when we experience resistance to this reading, typically in the form of disappointed expectations. If that was a flower, it should have a stem; if that was Helen, she should look thus and so on nearer approach – we experience resistance when our equally spontaneous readings a moment afterward do not fulfil the expectations set up by the earlier one. The parallel in experimental science is clear. Michelson and Morley *could have said*: if that was a measurement set-up to register light's speed in the ether, as we thought, then the readings should not have been the same at different times of year.

> I wish to walk a fine line here. What can be observed, and what there really is to be observed, is a matter of fact – it is not theory-, mind-, or language-dependent, but is there regardless of whether we even so much as pay attention to it. That is one side. On the other side, the question of

1 It is crucial, I think, to keep track of where we are using our common language and where we speak about that language. Nothing in the latter should contradict what I say in the former: that should be a criterion for philosophical discourse. If you or I says willingly such things as "I see a flower", without need in principle to qualify that, then we cannot when discussing language say that there is no fact of the matter as to whether I see a flower. That seems to me just a point of logic, and therefore needs no backing up with metaphysical theories.

> *what there is to be observed* is a question which in each of our mouths takes on the meaning of the language in which we live and breathe and have our being. (LE, p. 355)

In several papers below it is argued that I can not walk this fine line, that without some admixture of metaphysical realism I lose the world, I have no right to speak of the fact of the matter, or of truth, or of knowledge. I will do my best to counter those arguments.

1 Observability and the Epistemic Community

> We will argue that there is a tension between van Fraassen's claims, on the one hand, that observability is an objective matter of fact and, on the other hand, that observability is a function of the epistemic community. This is because membership in the epistemic community depends on moral and ideological criteria, so that observability in the last resort depends on these criteria, which do not seem to be objective. Therefore observability is not an objective property, either. (this volume, p. 35)

It is indeed crucial to constructive empiricism that observability is an objective property, in a pertinent sense, since otherwise the point of the position is moot. Empirical adequacy is, roughly speaking, truth about what is observable. Constructive empiricism, put in a nutshell, is that the criterion of success in science is not truth but empirical adequacy. Whether the criterion of success is met is meant to be something not determined by our moral or ideological commitments but by how things in the domain of the science are and behave.

But I must proceed very carefully here: the usage of "objective" varies greatly across contexts in philosophy (and elsewhere as well), so there is a danger that I might answer the letter of the argument and not its spirit. Briefly, I will respond that we must distinguish between the sense of "our epistemic community" and its reference, and for both of these, distinguish between what they are and how they may change (hence, what they are or could be at other times). I will argue, what is observable by the referent of "us" is indeed objective, in the sense required for constructive empiricism to be a non-trivial alternative.

1.1 Factual claims

I claim that my friend Ric has free-climbed a 5.11 route (Yosemite scale), and that I have not. Is that a factual claim, 'objective', or just the expression of a 'subjective' judgement? The former, I maintain.

Yet there are many remarks to be made about the concepts mobilized in this claim that have to do with values, norms, and decisions and that could not be settled 'merely by looking'. What distinguishes free climbing from aid climbing? That one climbs without the use of aids to advance, as opposed to aids that function only as protection and come into use only in an accident. But over the course of the last hundred years, many devices were introduced that are accepted as proper to free climbing that might not have been so accepted. To wear shoes with stealth rubber soles is OK – although after their introduction, people could climb routes that they could not climb before. The use of stealth rubber makes certain additional kinds of move possible at everyone's level of strength and skill. There was no official tribunal to decide that the climbing community accepts it; in some inexplicit way a decision was involved. Values played a role in that decision: that this practice counts as proper makes for a more interesting, exciting sport.[2]

The sense that "free climb" has at the moment is settled for now. That is why the question whether someone has free climbed a certain route is a factual question. A precondition for its being a factual question is certainly the requirement that the concepts mobilized are settled *at this time* in relevant respects. It was a great event in the climbing community when Lynn Hill freed the Nose route on El Capitan. Did she really? Her partner was of course

2 Alan Richardson gives the example of "castling" in chess – after a certain point this came to count as a legal move, and the value involved certainly had to do with what makes for "better" games, by criteria that did not derive from the official rules of chess as it was up to that point. I prefer to use climbing as an example because there, just as in science, success will not be determined solely by how well the players play – nature, beyond control, will have the last word.

watching her the entire time as he held the protecting rope – he knew what the criteria are and how to apply them – yes, she did. *That is a factual claim.* How the concepts became settled, how the terms acquired their current sense, and what is involved in changes to the sense of these or similar terms – all that is important in itself, but irrelevant to the factual status of the claim, at this point.

In the terms used by Wilfrid Sellars, John McDowell, and their compères, free climbing belongs to the space of reasons, the concept of a free climb is a norm-governed concept – in Ryle's earlier terms, "free-climb" is a success word. But given that the sense is settled in relevant respects at this time, the term has its proper use in claims that are simply as to the fact of the matter.

1.2 The factual claim of observability

The sense of "our epistemic community" has much to be said about it. The term "our" is an indexical – so the phrase is context-dependent, as are all phrases that include indexicals. The terms "epistemic" and "community", like "free-climb" are norm-governed. A new question as to whether or not a being or species is to count as part of our epistemic community, will in general involve a decision and not just 'merely looking to see what it is like'. Values will guide that decision; but even the question of which of our values will take precedence there will probably not be settled already beforehand.

But for the moment, the sense is settled sufficiently for present purposes, to let us say what is the referent of this phrase.

Similarly – in this context in which the referent is definite – the term "observable" has a definite referent. I do not mean that its sense has been spelled out sufficiently well as yet within philosophy of science, either by me or anywhere. I meant to make a good beginning in *The Scientific Image*, and this effort has been continued in ways that seem to me satisfactory as far as they go, and promising for the remainder.[3] We all know how to make the distinction in familiar cases: birds are visible and air is not, while air is tangible and

3 Cf. EPS, section 2 and pp. 284, 290, 297, 303-305; with Monton in CEMN; and Muller (2005).

magnetic fields are not, human song is audible and the bat's ultrasonic signals are not. In each case, as for "portable" and "potable" there is a tacit "to us", which means that their sense is indexical, but the reference is to the limits of the human perceptual organs, which are what they are as a matter of fact. A carefully spelled out explication of the concept must entail these examples as clear cases, if it is to be adequate at all.

1.3 Our epistemic community

The authors are quite right to complain that although I give some indications of what sorts of criteria could be involved in a decision as to membership in our epistemic community, I do not say what they are.[4] The indications I did give do imply, as they point out, that there would be moral and perhaps ideological considerations involved.[5] They suggest that trust must be an important factor, since in the sciences too, practice is such as to ride on trust in many respects. Trust, as they rightly say (referring to Seager's "Scientific Antirealism and the Epistemic Community"), involves a belief that the other is reliable in relevant respects. So in this case, one question would be "If we count the following signals as observation reports, are they reliable as such?" Given that the criteria for reliability in this context are clear, this will be – in context – a factual question.

But while many factual questions need to be answered in such a case, that is definitely not the end of the matter. When stealth rubber was introduced, there were of course factual questions of importance to the climbing community: how would the sport change in fact if that were accepted as proper free climbing? But by themselves, answers to these factual questions do not determine the decision. To make the point briefly: trust will be a very im-

4 There is a little more in *The Empirical Stance*, Lecture 5, sect. 8, but the point stands. As my student Daniel Herrick has urged, a human being has to meet several specific criteria to qualify, such as being able to express and communicate beliefs and perceptual judgements for example.

5 I prefer to say here "considerations involved"; I do not want to imply that there are rules and already definite criteria to settle the question. This point also brings us into a larger problem area in philosophy of course. My sympathies here lie with the particularism advocated in Dancy (2004) (similar lines of thought have occurred elsewhere of course, notably in Sartre's "Éxistentialism is a Humanism").

portant factor, but it does not consist simply in a factual belief as to reliability.[6]

This just underlines my agreement with the authors that there will be values, norms, and similar considerations involved – considerably more morally onerous and significant in the case of membership in the epistemic community than in the climbing community of course. But in all such cases, let us distinguish three questions:

1. How did our terms come to have the sense they now have – what was involved, if anything, beyond 'merely looking'?
2. How can the sense and reference of our terms change in the future – what will be involved, if anything, beyond 'merely looking'?
3. [Given the sense our terms now have] do they apply to such and such a case?

I place the "Given" in brackets in the last question, for it refers to what would be tacitly taken for granted, presupposed, in the context when such a question comes up in practice. And *there,* the question will be a purely factual one, regardless of how the first and second question are answered.

2 To be Prussian or not to be Prussian – van Fraassen and the Inference to the Best Explanation

This gives me a good opportunity to talk a bit about IBE in general, but also to respond specifically to these critiques of the 'best of a bad lot' argument and the 'argument from indifference'.[7]

I'll do three things. The first is to go a bit into the background, including the arguments that pertain more specifically to scientific realism in *The Scientific Image*. The second is to give my own response to those two arguments of-

6 See Holton (1994).

7 The latter were also targeted e.g. by Peter Lipton; see *Metascience* 14 (2005) symposium on his second edition of *Inference to the Best Explanation* (Lipton (2004)) for further commentary.

fered in *Laws and Symmetry* which are this paper's main target.[8] And then finally I'll suggest that even after all this, the upshot of this discussion cannot be seen to hold out any hope of support for scientific realism through IBE.

2.1 Initial arguments using IBE in support of scientific realism

In Ch. 2 of *The Scientific Image* the focus is on uses of IBE in support of scientific realism.[9] The first argument is about the following

> Claim: we all use this rule in 'ordinary' every-day cases.

This claim is made on the basis of observed inferential behavior: we notice cases in which a person observes something and forms a conclusion that goes beyond his data, and notice that his way of doing this is in accord with IBE. I'll take for granted that there are indeed many cases like that. But does that fact support the Claim?

This behavior fits many rules – most trivially, the rule to infer q from p, with no restrictions.

Of course that rule is so bad that it would lead to inconsistency. But there are other rules that it fits. Suppose for example, if the conclusion is a hypothesis about observable entities. For this case, empirical adequacy and truth coincide. Therefore the general rule followed might be to infer (not to the truth) but to the empirical adequacy of the best explanation.

The important point here is that the Claim is itself an inference, which selects one explanation (of the observed behavior) among others.

One notices of course that the support offered of IBE would be circular if that selection was based on an evaluation of it as selecting the best explanation! The argument here is not meant as advocacy of a rule of inference to the empirical adequacy of the best explanation. In my view, any such rule would be open to serious objections. The point is rather that the move from the offered basis of the Claim to the Claim is itself without the support it needs.

8 That I had such a response I "own[ed] up immediately" in reaction to David Armstrong's "I take it that van Fraassen is having a bit of fun here"; LS, p. 147.

9 Cf. SI, sect. 3 (pp. 19-23).

It is remarkable that advocates of IBE have not offered better support for it. David Armstrong made the most sustained attempt to do so.[10] Everyone engages, according to Armstrong, in induction, and this needs justification – Hume's famous problem. But a justification is forthcoming: in the end it rests on IBE. That is where the demand for justification ends, however, and he writes simply:

> If making such an inference is not rational, what is?
> To infer to the best explanation is part of what it is to be rational. If that is not rational, what is?[11]

2.2 The 'best of a bad lot' argument

I started with this in that same section in *The Scientific Image*: even if we grant the scientific realist the use of IBE, s/he needs an extra premise to make it apply. For the rule can only apply after we have selected a range of explanations, from which the best is to be chosen. That selection can be biased – the premise needed is that it is not biased. For example, when it is suggested that we should apply this rule in the case of rival scientific theories, a realist might take the option to be a choice of which of the theories is true, whereas his opponent might take the option to be a choice of which of them is empirically adequate.

But this point is needlessly specific here. The use of IBE starts with specifying a range of explanations of the given phenomena or data, to which this rule of theory choice is to be applied. The first remark we may make here is that this range, of "serious options" will typically be limited peculiarly, in a practical context of inquiry, differing from one research community to another. But even if the rule is applied to the entire range of historically given (constructed) hypotheses or theories, that range is limited. Since the rule is one that is 'inductive', i.e. to lead to conclusions that go beyond the evidence,

10 An attempt I criticize in LS, Ch. 6, sect. 3.

11 Armstrong (1983), p. 53 and 59. I have offered an answer to these rhetorical questions partly in Chapter 7 of LS and partly in FHT.

there is no guarantee that this range contains a true hypothesis. So the use of IBE may in fact be a case of choosing the best of a bad lot.

Apel et al. reconstruct this argument, to some extent following Psillos, as an argument to the conclusion that we are not justified in the assumption that the best available explanation is likely to be true, hinging on the premise that we cannot rule out the possibility that all explanations [in the given range] are false. This notion of justification or warrant plays a central role in what I called *defensive epistemology*, so I can't say that I would have cast the argument in such terms myself. (cf. LS, pp. 170, 186) My own conclusion did not go much further than I had gone in the initial point:

> [IBE] requires a step beyond the comparative judgment that this hypothesis is better than its actual rivals. While the comparative judgment is indeed a 'weighing (in the light of) the evidence', the extra step – let us call it the ampliative step – is not. For me to take it that the best of set *X* will be more likely to be true than not, requires a prior belief that the truth is already more likely to be found in *X*, than not. (LS, p. 143)

That is, coherence requires the user of IBE in a given case to have that opinion – this is a precondition for its use, which the scientific realist writers had ignored.

This already introduces my own reaction to the 'best of a bad lot' argument. The argument is simply a pointer to one of the conditions of coherence for any individual, specific case of (apparent) application of the rule. It is only one condition, still quite weak; it is not enough but it is certainly needed.

2.3 The 'argument from indifference'

I believe, and so do you, that there are many theories, perhaps never yet formulated but in accordance with all evidence so far, which explain at least as well as the best we have now. Since these theories can disagree in so many ways about statements that go beyond our evidence to date, it is clear that most of them by far must be false. I know nothing about our best explanation, relevant to its truth-value, except that it belongs to this class. So I must treat it as a random member of this class, most of which is false. Hence it must seem very improbable to me that it is true. (cf. LS, p. 146)

That is how I presented this argument. Apel et al. reconstruct it as involving the premise that all members of this class are equally likely to be true. They are quite right to point the finger there, but note that I did not insert a factual premise, but rather a rule of inference of the same general sort as IBE:

> I know nothing about our best explanation, relevant to its truth-value, except that it belongs to this class. So I must treat it as a random member of this class, most of which is false.

We can immediately see that this is contentious, for it is a rule to apply a sort of principle of indifference, of the sort that has encountered so many difficulties in logical interpretations of probability. So Apel and others very reasonably and rightly bring up the pertinent considerations that echo those difficulties:

> In an anti-Prussian spirit van Fraassen could stick to the original version of his argument and defend the first premise as follows: Every claim is innocent until proved guilty. Therefore the assumption that there are always many equally good unborn rivals to the best available explanation does not stand in need of justification anymore.
>
> But this reasoning will not do. First of all, we could make a similar move for the denial of van Fraassen's premise. One could say: Unless there are reasons to the contrary it is justified to assume that there are *not* many good unborn explanations. We are caught in a deadlock. (this volume, p. 53)

But if we take that into account, we can once again see a pointer to a condition of coherence. Users of IBE must take note of what they themselves see as the range of alternatives, whether already historically formulated or not, and must declare that it seems unlikely to them that the truth is to be found among the unconsidered alternatives.

This does not go much beyond the coherence condition already noted above, if at all. But it takes us automatically, as it were, to the considerations that could be mentioned in elaborating on this good opinion about the actual range of choice. For once we are settled there, the rule bids us go for the more explanatory – the 'lovelier' as Lipton likes to say. And then the obvious question is: do the lovelier ones seem likelier to you, for that very reason? Coherence then requires specifying what makes them lovelier – unless that already has so definite a meaning that we can all tell how to apply it – and expressing or at least having an opinion according to which hypotheses with these characteristics are more likely to be true.

In none of this does it seem to me a requirement that the person who makes up his or her mind in this fashion has a justification. I ask only for coherence in the state of opinion, for the pursuit of coherence, as opposed to justification, does seem to me to be a requirement of (epistemic) rationality. That, of course, is the point of citing Justice Oliver Wendel Holmes on the difference between the Prussian and English concept of law.

Now it should be clear how I respond myself to those two arguments. As stated they are at best thoroughly misleading. They do not show that IBE is not to be trusted; they bring out the conditions of coherence to be satisfied in any specific case in which someone changes his or her opinion in a way that accords with IBE. If those conditions are satisfied, there is no objection left.[12]

2.4 Do we now have succor to offer the scientific realist?

As stated, I just said, these two infamous arguments are at best thoroughly misleading. But in saying this, I was speaking from my own point of view, which is the anti-Prussian one (as one might say) in epistemology. There are no ampliative rules of inference, coherence is all. From that point of view, what sort of support could a scientific realist get from reflections on IBE?

There are two sorts of apparent good applications of this rule that the scientific realist likes to discuss. The first is in cases of theory choice or hypothesis choice in the sciences. Accepted scientific opinion today is at variance with much of scientific opinion as it was say 50 or 100 years ago. It must

12 Apel et al. explicitly stay away from the argument of the next chapter that goes further into conditions of coherence; see further the next note.

be possible to view the change as rational. *We are all agreed, I think, that this is indeed possible*, and not just on the pretense that it was just a matter of deduction from (or conditionalizing on) the new evidence added to what was believed before. I view it as changes that were permissible made under conditions where the actors were throughout epistemically rational. If any scientific realists wish to go further and adopt a 'Prussian' point of view, insisting that it was rational only if the change was rationally compelled, by rules of right reason, then it seems to me the onus is on them. They will indeed face the 'justification of induction' problem, and prior to that, the formulation of coherent inductive policies that do include ampliative rules of inference. In my opinion the problem based on a mistake, and coherent inductive policies cannot include such ampliative rules, though they need not preclude ampliation in practice.[13]

2.5 The 'no miracle argument' – how the realist begs the question

The second application that scientific realists like is in the so-called 'no miracle argument' in support of scientific realism. Thus John Worrall, in his opening sally for the proposal of structural realism:

> The main argument for scientific realism is that our present theories in science are so successful empirically that they could not have gotten that way by chance – instead they must somehow have latched on to the blueprint of the universe.[14]

13 At the end of their paper Apel et al. express puzzlement about how this is possible – how an epistemic policy could allow for ampliation in practice while eschewing any ampliative rules of inference. Since they do not elaborate, I'll just refer to LS Ch. 7, section 5 "Sketch for an epistemology". In the light of that I would add: there is therefore no objection left for someone who makes that sort of move on a particular occasion, while satisfying those conditions of coherence – but we have to distinguish this from someone who adopts IBE as a rule for changing opinion. To adopt it as a rule (as opposed to occasionally behaving in a way that is in accordance with it) does lead one inexorably into incoherence. That is the reflection that makes it possible to "give room to practices of ampliation beyond the evidence" (LS, p. 151), which Apel et al. query. I would like to explore this further through ethics rather than law, e.g. in relation to Jonathan Dancy's *Ethics Without Principles* (2004).

14 Worrall (1989), p. 99.

Is this an argument? We can clearly see two ingredients: a demand for explanation, in this case of the success of science overall, and secondly a conclusion. That conclusion is hard to see as anything but an offered explanation, presumably one better than any other candidate.

It can't very well be a scientific explanation, for scientific explanations we do have, and can have, of success in science draw on later or different scientific theories. For example, physics today offers a good explanation of the success of Newtonian physics, within the limits of its application, in its first two centuries of existence. In general, on the basis of (the assumption of empirical adequacy of) later or current accepted theories we can explain the (limited) success of earlier theories. The no miracle argument does not belong to this range of possible explanations of the past successes of science. It purports to have an explanation of the successful career of science as a whole, so there is no further scientific theory for it to draw on. So it is not a scientific explanation. It is an offer of an explanation, and takes this explanation as to be accepted as true, on the basis of its explanatory success in this respect.

Let us try to evaluate that. Since it is not a scientific explanation, it is very reasonable to ask just what its content is, and what its credentials are. As to content we can quote the initial formulation due to Boyd and Putnam:

> […] the positive argument for realism is that it is the only philosophy that doesn't make the success of science a miracle. That terms in mature scientific theories typically refer (this formulation is due to Richard Boyd), that the theories accepted in a mature science are typically approximately true, that the same term can refer to the same thing even when it occurs in different theories – these statements are viewed by the scientific realist not as necessary truths but as part of the only scientific explanation of the success of science, and hence as part of any adequate scientific description of science and its relations to its objects.[15]

The "hence" at the end is the mark of an inference – 'these statements' are part of the only (and so the best) explanation, hence are true.

15 Putnam (1975), p. 73.

In view of our preceding discussion we must now point out that the person applying IBE here must, to be coherent, already be of the opinion that the selected range of explanations contains the truth. Since here the range has only one member, it follows that coherence requires belief in its truth before the rule is applied – but then the rule is redundant, it arrives at no more than what was needed for its application, it begs the question.

This could be fixed, by striking Putnam's exuberant "only", and adding rival explanations of the success of science, so as to have a range to which to apply IBE. When we try to explore this however, we find a further disconnect between the participants in the dialogue, and in the end the scientific realist is still begging the question. The exploration goes into two directions.

First, we note that what is to be explained is the historical success of science. The scientific realist may begin with "because it is true", and the empiricist with "because it is empirically adequate". Of course both are too strong – truth and even empirical adequacy is what science is striving for. So both qualify: because mature scientific theories approach the truth (respectively, empirical adequacy) and have achieved some approximation thereto, in relevant respects. Fine, but now the realist retorts to the empiricist "Yours is not an explanation – what you say is precisely what has to be explained!"

We have here a good illustration of the discussion of the erotetic view of explanation.[16] What the 'Why?' question asks for is determined by the questioner, who in effect requests a selection from a very specific (though often only vaguely indicated) range of answers. Here we see that the realists' range of possible answers to the why-question, what accounts for the success of science overall, contains only ones that make claims going beyond empirical adequacy. Once again, since the use of IBE requires as precondition a belief that truth is to be found in the specified range, this begs the question if used in argument on behalf of scientific realism.

In *The Scientific Image* I tried a different tack: the Darwinian response "Do not be surprised to see such highly successful theories today – unsuccessful ones died through natural selection in the scientific community!" Just as we should not be surprised that mice flee from cats: kinds that did not are no longer with us.

16 As advocated in SI, Ch. 5.

Here realists reply once more that this sort of response does not answer the question as meant. For the mouse one wants a further explanation too, namely of the mechanism in brain, glands, nerves, and muscles that constitute the flight response, and in addition the mechanism by which that flight response is inherited. Similarly then, it is not enough, or not even relevant, to say that today we have successful theories because scientists kept culling and replacing ones they found inadequate. In addition, we must have an account of why these specific surviving theories succeed in the business of empirical prediction.

To this request, if really made about a specific theory, we can get scientific answers, based *on more comprehensive or later* theories. Thus molecular biology holds out the hope of accounting for the success of population genetics, and physics for the success of molecular biology. If we try for an explanation of science as a whole, we are thrown back from science onto metaphysics, with its properties, propositions, propensities, possible alternative worlds, causation and causal nexus, disposition, reduction, supervenience, and so forth, or, at a minimum, a claim of truth made in the context of a correspondence theory of truth. The why-question, as meant, requests selection from a range of answers none of which make sense to the empiricist. Presuming that this why-question must have a true direct answer begs the question in the scientific realist-empiricist debate.

3 THE HARDSHIPS OF AN EMPIRICIST – VAN FRAASSEN'S COMPROMISE BETWEEN EPISTEMIC MODESTY AND ADEQUACY TO SCIENCE

> The paper deals with two central features of Bas van Fraassen's overall empiricist project, namely epistemic modesty and adequacy to science. After clarifying these two notions, we will try to show that there is a serious tension between the two requirements. Moreover, we interpret constructive empiricism as a compromise between them and argue that it is an unsatisfying one. (this volume, p. 57)

By epistemic modesty the authors say they mean "refraining from far-reaching metaphysical speculations", which is indeed a central feature of the empiricist stance. Adequacy to science refers here to the *portrayal* of science – science being a vast enterprise involving many actors and practices throughout many centuries so far, and portrayed differently in constructive empiricism than in other philosophical currents. Names are always tricky: "constructive empiricism" is of course not the name of a sort of empiricism, but closely related: it names a view of science which I present as eminently "congenial to the empiricist standpoint", as they rightly point out.

3.1 Empiricists' stake in the portrayal of science

Why is there a tension between the two? One could refrain from metaphysical speculation oneself while portraying scientists as engaged in rampant metaphysical speculation. But that would not sit well with another crucial aspect of the empiricist stance: the centrality of admiration for the empirical sciences in that stance. So the empiricist has a strong motive for portraying science as not requiring involvement in metaphysics.

That is certainly true, and similarly a metaphysician has some stake in the idea that such a widely admired intellectual and practical enterprise has 'metaphysical foundations' and is not adequately conceivable without them. Similarly, when inference to the best explanation is the vehicle by which alone metaphysicians can be carried to their conclusions, they have a stake in portraying science as propelled by the same vehicle. When causation is the metaphysicians' cement of the universe they have a motive to tell the story of science as a search for causal explanations of natural phenomena.

Given all that, we clearly all have a stake in finding ways to evaluate portrayals of science, answers to the question 'what is science?', that are sufficiently independent of our philosophical allegiances to allow for dialogue.

3.2 The scientists' pursuit of truth

> It might be objected, however, that CE provides a rather misleading portrayal of what science is after. Isn't it on closer inspection simply a fact that science as a social venture aims at providing true theories, theories

> that depict reality more or less correctly with respect to its observable and its unobservable domain? (this volume, p. 60)

Such facts are not, it seems to me, accessible to casual inspection or simple questioning. What would closer inspection bring to light? In closer inspection we should of course heed the lesson Kant said we learned from Galileo: that nature must be 'put to the question', that it must be subject to testing of our own design – that, in effect, the facts come to light only with pain. The paper rightly points out, in its final section, that I "[do] not equate the aim of science with what scientists take to be the aim of their professional doings". But I do think the defining aim of their enterprise will have telling signs in what may come out in appropriately sensitive and sophisticated testing. So I suggest that to see whether science as a social venture aims at the truth about the unobservable, we have to raise difficulties.

One bit of recent history that I think is telling is the difference in reactions to Bohm's hidden variable interpretation of quantum theory ('Bohmian mechanics'). Philosophers are fascinated. The logical tenability of this version shows that it was simply not true that the quantum theory implies that particles cannot have continuous well defined spatio-temporal trajectories – as was often asserted by physicists. So the very existence of Bohm's theory is a challenge to the conventional wisdom among scientists. But are the physicists interested? I think the response I got from one working physicist was typical. After I explained how Bohm's ideas work, and how they were put on a solid mathematical footing, he asked: "Can any experiments be designed that would help us to decide between quantum mechanics with its usual interpretation, and Bohmian mechanics?" Of course I had to answer No, Bohmian mechanics says that the world is quite different, but its empirical predictions are the same. He laughed a little and said, "well, then I think they should just take it home and play with it". The truth of the matter, whether the unobservable processes are one way or the other, evoked no interest.

We cannot put too much weight on such anecdotes. Physicists are usually not philosophers, they usually have neither the same concerns nor the sort of training that places them inside the philosophical dialogue. An astrophysicist, also thinking about Bohmian mechanics, told me "if they have the same empirical predictions, if no conceivable experiment can bring out a difference, then they are the same theory". I said they couldn't be the same, since they contradict each other about what nature is really like. Oh well, he said, they are the same in every way that really matters.

A philosopher who says something like that has to spell out what this equivalence is. My reply is that it is empirical equivalence, in the sense I gave that in *The Scientific Image*, and my view of science is that this is indeed sameness in every way that really matters in the end. But unlike my astrophysicist friend, I strongly qualify that: there are many pragmatic virtues and considerations that rightly play a role in theory choice in scientific practice. He was right, I think, only in the sense that the truth pursued is just truth about what is observable. But that is an awful lot of truth to pursue.

3.3 A footnote to epistemic false modesty

If the driving force of empiricism were to believe as little as possible, empiricists might indeed have a motive to portray science as only pursuing the truth about what is observed during the span of human history. Sans antecedent, sans subjunctive, this seems to be Marc Alspector-Kelly's contention. I see no real connection between this idea and the empiricist tradition, so the point is moot as far as I am concerned.

Nor does it have any connection to what we see happening in science. When Halley predicted the return of his comet, was that to be understood as having the rider "if we live that long"? If we do not have a firm belief about what our future holds, our predictions must be taylored to what we think *can* happen, not to what we think *will* happen.

3.4 The other challenge

The authors join Psillos and McMullin in arguing that my rejection of traditional epistemological 'principles of right reason' precludes an account of science as solidly based on empirical evidence. If that is so, the internal tension in CE surely rips it apart:

> Wouldn't it be strange to determine the aim of science as giving us empirically adequate theories, if we never had any conclusive evidence for a theory's being empirically adequate? (this volume, pp. 64f.)

That would at least be as strange as determining the aim of science to be a true account of the unobservable, while insisting that we can never have any conclusive evidence for a theory's yielding precisely that.

I do not mean this last remark as a criticism of the scientific realist. I don't suppose that "conclusive evidence" was meant very strictly here. Lord Kelvin had conclusive evidence that the earth could not be more than some tenths of millions of years old – conclusive in the context of what was then accepted science. The evidence was of course not conclusive in a wider historical context. The serious question is rather whether, on my grounds, I can say at all that the evidence favors one theory over another with respect to empirical adequacy. *A theory is not empirically adequate unless it covers as well the relevant future phenomena, at present unknown.* To maintain that it does, must one not rely on Induction, Abduction, Inference to the Best Explanation?

I do not think so – I think that the traditional epistemology which offers us an account of right reason in terms of such rules and the picture of ampliative-rule-following is both illogical and unrealistic, for scientific as well as 'ordinary' intellectually responsible deliberation. In a given context, evidence appears, is received, and is classified as such, in the frame of a prior communal opinion, and is accommodated so as to form a responsive posterior opinion. This management of the community's opinion in response to communal experience is to some extent by logic and to some extent by a form of practical decision-making (that certainly involves risk-taking as well as prudence).[17]

17 There is so much more to be said on this topic – I'll just refer here to LS, Chapter 7 and my FHTE.

4 Experience Becoming Fully Literate: van Fraassen On The Verge Of Constructivism

> We suspect that it is van Fraassen's strong loyalty to the project of empiricism and parts of its history, especially to the search for a fundament of all knowledge in experience, that makes him come to a purportedly sustainable compromise. On the one hand he readily accepts a nearly all-embracing theory- and language-dependence of experience, on the other he clings to a realistic understanding of observability and observation as the cornerstones of empiricism. But if this compromise leads to inconsistency, wouldn't it be more promising for van Fraassen to leave his "fine line" and take sides with constructivism altogether? (this volume, p. 79)

I am especially happy to have this challenge, based on a combined reading of *The Scientific Image,* parts of "From vicious circle to infinite regress, and back again", and "Literate Experience: The [De-, Re-] Interpretation of Nature". There has always been a general impression that to accept the view that language is theory-laden, and that even our judgements in direct perceptual response are couched in our theory-laden language, leads one inexorably into an extreme form of relativism or constructivism. (The authors of this paper seem sufficiently sympathetic to constructivism not to equate it with a debilitating skepticism – many who see the same inexorable slide are quick to do so.) But I am convinced that there is no such inexorable slide from one into the other, and that those who slide are prey to a confusion.

4.1 The two faces of experience

Experience is Janus-faced. What I experience is what happens to me, of which I am aware. But when I say or judge or think what it is that I experienced, I will frame the judgment in the language I have, my language in use. Even after realizing that my language is theory-laden I do not for one moment think that there is no right or wrong to my judging, or that what I sincerely assert is not so. I do not think so for a moment! For I assert sincerely only what I take to be true. I may think so a moment later ... or at least succumb to doubt and submit my own recent opinion to test – but that too presupposes that it could have been true, and that there are ways to test that.

A perceptual judgement, in the sense of an immediate response to experience, may be wrong. In retrospect we can point to many examples. In the dark I tripped over a skunk, but I took it to be the cat; my perceptual judgment was "I tripped over a cat", and that was false. It may be recognizably theory-laden. Perhaps I feel heat and think spontaneously that some phlogiston is escaping nearby – having been educated thoroughly in the phlogiston theory. This is, in my context, the correct response; I have been conditioned to make immediate judgements of this form in response to this feeling. To resist the 'myth of the given' is precisely to deny that there is a prior proposition evident to me that is not couched in my theory-laden language, for which my judgement is an interpretation. Later on, having gone over to the oxidation theory of combustion I realize that my earlier immediate responses carried false theoretical implications. But I also remember that I made those responses usually at just the right time. Usually but not always – sometimes I was mistaken, in the sense that I needed to correct myself: what happened was not a being heated but say, a sudden onset of fever. Remembering those self-corrections I do not now reject them, but I represent the situation differently: "At that time I used to say 'phlogiston is escaping nearby' to indicate nearby combustion – and sometimes I would say that mistakenly, e.g. when I was becoming feverish".

One thing is clear here: in my later story about myself I certainly do not say that I failed to perceive what was happening, though now I say that my perceptual judgements carried false theoretical implications.

4.2 Metaphysical realism contested

Labels for philosophical positions are a treacherous brood. In the context of our present discussion, it seems to me that there are two topics under the heading of my rejection of metaphysical realism. In both cases, the challenge is to show how I can maintain the cited assertions:

> What nature is like does not depend on what our experience or representation of nature is like. (LE, 354)

> What can be observed, and what there really is to be observed, is a matter of fact – it is not theory-, mind-, or language-dependent, but is there regardless of whether we even so much as pay attention to it. (LE, 355)

In the preceding section I have elaborated on these, and indicated some lines of defence. But what I have to face explicitly is the authors' contention that these assertions imply the very doctrines that I reject elsewhere as metaphysical postulates.

What I shall now argue is that this contention rests on an view of language, reference, and truth that is itself solidly encased in metaphysical realism, and that this view is by no means the only way to understand ourselves. But there are two points to be discussed separately. The first is the 'reification' of structure in nature, and the second is representation in language.

4.2.1 Reification of structure

> According to van Fraassen, an advocate of metaphysical realism claims that, while observing, one is able to catch a glimpse of what the structure of nature is really like (LE, 347f.), i.e. of "properties, attributes, Universals, Relations – in short, [of the] real structure present in the things" (LE, 347) themselves which are completely independent of any judging and classifying activity of the observer. (this volume, p. 70)

As is pointed out here, I reject such a view. What I reject is the metaphysical position that 'reifies', that is, that postulates entities in nature to underpin our classifications and thereby provide 'truthmakers' for our judgements. Consider the contrast between

a. The apple is red.
b. There is a property that the apple has, namely redness.

The realist contention is that a. can be true only if, and because, b. (or a similar posit) is true. The existence of the property, and its instantiation by the individual, explains the conditions under which a predication can be true. But as Quine pointed out in his "On What There Is", the first sentence implies the existence of an apple, and not of anything else, while the second implies the existence of two entities, an apple and a property. From this it follows that the first does not logically imply the second. Therefore, to deny the second does not deny that the apple is red.

The crucial point is that as far as logic is concerned, neither properties, nor universals, nor any other postulated entities to provide truthmakers, need to exist for apples to be red, or for such sentences to be true. What about the realist contention that they are needed to *explain* how apples can be red, or how sentences can be true? Well, what is the demand for explanation that is insistently advanced here, and how is it satisfied? If it is unqualified, then the truth of b. stands as much in need of explanation as a., and a further postulate is needed – an old familiar regress. It is not inconsistent to postulate that there is an infinitely regressing series of explainers that really exist ... but then, where is the satisfaction that explanation is meant to provide? An explanation satisfies when it 'closes the door' on a question, when it removes wonder. But in this case no doors are ever closed.

But there must be a reason why the sentence is true! Yes, indeed there is: the reason is that the apple is red. And that is all.

4.2.2 The one true story of the world

How are languages theory-laden? They are theory-laden because the predicates express a classification, and a classification derives typically at least in part from a theory that provides the taxonomy (as Duhem insightfully emphasized). We can see this infection by theory in a dictionary; here is one example:

> *radio*, n.
>
> I. 1. A message sent by wireless telegraphy or telephony; a radiotelegram. *Obs.*

> II. 2. a. The transmission and reception of radio-frequency electromagnetic waves, esp. as a means of communication that does not need a connecting wire; wireless telephony or telegraphy. (Oxford English Dictionary)

We do not need to perform tests, even if we knew how, to check whether the object that wakes me with music in the morning is receiving electromagnetic waves, in order to use the word "radio" today. No understanding or knowledge of electromagnetism is required for this use; nor any belief in the reality of electromagnetic fields. But relative to our accepted physical theory this object is classified as a receiver, processor, and amplifier of electromagnetic waves, and this is part of the meaning of the word "radio" that we use.

Such a taxonomy can get us into trouble, precisely because reliance on the theory may not be vindicated – at the point where anomalies appear and scientists work on replacing that theory. Perhaps it was once part of the meaning of "cat", "mouse", "horse" that the predicate applied to parents only if it also applied to their offspring. If so, our own words were shouting us down, to use Bacon's phrase, when a theory of evolution was proposed. The words needed to have their meanings changed or be replaced altogether, if our discourse were not to be fatally hampered. But as you can see from the word "radio", our use in practice can ride for a long time on old meanings; it will be a while before the Oxford English Dictionary has to adapt to the language of quantum electrodynamics.

What is the hallmark of a 'good' language? A language is the language of a community, if it is a living language at all; and it is good if it serves well in the practices of that community. This criterion is thoroughly empirical and pragmatic. Note that it is not entirely up to the community whether it has a good language – at some point its language ceases to serve well, and needs changing, and this comes unexpectedly, and certainly not by choice. Whether the language is a good language certainly depends on what language has evolved in the community's history, and on the practices it has developed – but does not depend entirely on those factors alone. By saying this we acknowledge the role of nature, of nature's response to our practice. And here we find the independence.

Once we take for granted the language we have, and keep fixed the fact that this is our language, we can say: whether our sentences are true is not up to us, whether something is a radio or not, is entirely independent of how we classify that thing, or what locus in our classification the word "radio" labels. Is this an overstatement? No. It looks inconsistent at first blush, but not on a second look. For consider:

> Our word "radio" could have been a word for electric hairdryers. If I own one radio and three hairdryers now, how many radios would I have owned if our word "radio" had been a word for hairdryers?

This is an old saw – the answer is ONE. It is sheer use/mention confusion to think otherwise.

But let us return to the insistent urgings of the metaphysical instinct. Given the way nature is there must be a language whose predicates derive from a taxonomy that is guaranteed never to run into trouble, no matter what our practices will be. The set of true sentences in that language is the one true story of the world. Our languages are good only to the extent that they mirror aspects of that one language whose predicates "carve nature at the joints".

That bit of reasoning starts well enough – by indicating something that appears to be logically possible. But even if that is so, the logical leap occurs with the word "one". If we have pointed here to a genuine logical possibility, there is no basis for thinking it unique. There are as logical possibilities many empirically equivalent theories, and thus many languages incarnating those theories' very different taxonomies in their predicate structure – the *one true story of the world* is an Illusion of Reason.

4.3 Observability is a matter of fact

Whether the apple is red depends on the meanings of "apple" and "red" in one sense, but not in the sense that makes us unrealistic. The dependence is just this: If the meanings of these words were different then so would be the truth conditions for the sentence "the apple is red". But the relevant independence is this: If he apple is red, then it would still have been red if the meanings of these words had been different.

The same applies to the word "observable" and our classification of things into observable and unobservable. Yes, different theories could disagree on which sorts of things are observable. If they also differ on what could ever be encountered in experience they might even work equally well as guides to practice. In that respect, there is no difference between "observable" and "water", for example. But speaking my own language, there is no ambiguity in my predication of "is observable", any more than in my predication of "is water".[18]

5 Indexical Truth and Anti-Metaphysical Inclinations – Getting Rid of the Remnants of Realism

> In some of [van Fraassen's] earlier writings the term 'truth' has a quite substantial ring to it; truth of a scientific theory, so it seems, is construed as correspondence of that theory to the world [...]. At other places, mostly in his more recent publications, [...] the notion of truth is taken to be tacitly indexical to our own language. Thus [...] it is a relation between scientific theories and statements in which *we* describe the world as it is represented *by us* [...].
> In the third section we will show that the two readings of 'true' are incompatible. We will suggest that if van Fraassen's claims in his more recent writings are to be taken seriously then he must also give up the last remnants of realism in his theory [...]. [Hence] van Fraassen – his intentions to the contrary – lands himself in idealism or pragmatism. (this volume, pp. 81f.)

This paper continues the strong challenge begun in the preceding one. The crucial question it poses for me is indeed whether my current views on truth do land me in idealism or pragmatism. The less interesting question is whether I really drastically changed my mind with respect to language and

18 There is more argument to this extent in the relevant section of VC and if that was not as clear as it should have been, I hope that what I have written here will make it valuable to go back there for a second look.

truth over the years – but it is of some interest to me, so I will begin with that.

5.1 Truth as I used to think of it

> For truth has such a face and such a mien, As to be lov'd needs only to be seen. (Dryden, *The Hind and the Panther*)

In *The Scientific Image*, whenever the notion of truth came up, I wrote in terms characteristic of correspondence views. Mea culpa! Rosenhagen is entirely right about this, and clearly documents the painful truth. The book is polemical, and some of my obliviousness there to possible implications of metaphysical baggage may be written off to an attempt to meet the scientific realist as far as possible on his own ground – if only for the sake of argument. But as Rosenhagen points out, I used the words "without demur, without putting any additional constraints on its usage" (note 3). I made no effort to put some distance between myself and such blatantly realist jargon as "I would still identify truth of a theory with the condition that there is an exact correspondence between reality and one of its [i.e. the theory's] models."

This is all the more disturbing to me, as I read it now, because I was a student of Wilfrid Sellars, and therefore well acquainted with the issues surrounding this topic, as well as sympathetic to Sellars' views on them.

But before I show too much contrition, let me try to put this book in the context of things I had been thinking and writing before 1980 that were more directly concerned with philosophy of language. Truth, like reference, is a technical term in semantics, which is the study of language in relation to the world – or, if that is too grandiose a way to put it, of expressions in relation to what they are about, and to each other. But what is the status of semantics?

> When we ask for an interpretation of a semantic concept, we may merely be requesting a definition in terms of other semantic concepts. In this sense, the question will not apply to the simpler, more basic concept of the discipline. We cannot take exception to the claim of semantics to have its own technical concepts. But this does not rule out the continued demand for an interpretation of these concepts: in that case, however,

> answers which go outside semantics proper must be acceptable. Such a demand for interpretation can only be construed as a request that we show the concepts in question to have a significant role.
> There is in fact an obvious field which may provide such a grounding for semantic concepts, namely, pragmatics. And I propose accordingly that we construe the demand for an interpretation of semantic concepts as answerable by the exhibition of a clear pragmatic counterpart. (MRAP, pp. 166-7)[19]
>
> The use of the semantic concept signals a certain level of abstraction, which involves disregarding the vagaries of contextual factors, idiosyncratic usage, changes in usage with time, and so on.[20] But had the concept of denotation no clear pragmatic counterpart, its use would have no clear relevance to the study of language at all. (ibid.)

In a follow-up I wrote:

> The use of a concept in formal semantics is at once warranted and of philosophical interest if and only if the concept has a clear pragmatic counterpart. And we call the second concept a pragmatic counterpart of the first if the first is arrived at from the second by abstraction from relations to user and to context of use. (MRM, closing paragraph).

My guiding example was "the semantic statement 'The term W denotes the object O' has as pragmatic counterpart 'The person X uses the term W to refer to the object O (at time t)'." For *truth* the similar point would then be that the semantic statement "Sentence S is true" has as pragmatic counterpart "The person X makes a true assertion by use of sentence S (at time t)". But what is it to make a true assertion? Here Sellars (whose views on semantics are cited as source in both articles) insisted on our providing 'cash value' for

19 This and MRM (see below) are cited in Ch. 6, section 5 of SI, which deals briefly with issues in philosophy of language.

20 Cf. Church's review of Nielsen's disparagement of such abstraction, *The Journal of Symbolic Logic* XXVII (1962), p. 118 (footnote in original).

such generalities in essentially Tarskian terms: if the sentence S is a sentence in our language, we must 'disquote' it to spell this out. For example,

> X makes a true assertion by use of "Snow is white" if and only if snow is white.

This will only work well if the context of X's use is the same as the context of use of this long sentence itself of course. We can't very well offer as an instance

> X makes a true assertion by use of "I am happy" if and only if I am happy

except for a context in which that is said by X himself – and so forth.

Although *The Scientific Image* introduced pragmatics (Chapter 5, section 4, especially 4.1), that discussion did not enter upon the status of semantics, or the implications for the concepts of truth and reference. But it does refer to an earlier place where I did so (nl. ONVN). There I was at pains to distinguish two things that could be meant by saying that a sentence is true in some other context, or under other circumstances, than my own:

a. S, as understood *here*, is true of situation β.
b. S is true in situation β, that is, true of β as understood in β.

Medieval examples such as "There are no sentences" had been on my mind since this discussions with Richmond Thomason, Robert Stalnaker, and Charles Daniels at Yale in the late sixties.[21] That sentence has no explicit indexicals or demonstratives in it, yet the above distinction is crucial: it is true of some conceivable world, but it could not be a true English sentence in any world in which it exists. So it is *tacitly indexical.*

What do we mean if we simply say that S is true? If we abstract from "S, as understood here, is true of situation β" which is on the level of pragmatics,

21 The medieval examples were a stimulus for work on the Liar and other such 'semantic' paradoxes, on which I was also writing at the time.

to form "S is true of situation β" – thus by 'ascending' to the level of semantics and thereby introducing truth as a semantic concept – we are ignoring or keeping fixed the contextual parameters. Now, if we simultaneously fix on our own context + situation, then we arrive at the usual use of "true": S is true simpliciter in situation β precisely if S, as understood in β, is true of β. When we say "S is true" we mean that S is true simpliciter in our own situation.

It was indeed only much later that I began to see how the deliberate ignorance exercised in this abstraction, ensconced in our love for remaining on that abstract level, leads the unwary philosopher into metaphysical quandaries.

5.2 What I think about truth now

... does not go much beyond the above, it seems to me. What are typically cited as basic principles concerning truth, reference, and other semantic matters are typically pragmatic tautologies. That is, their formulations in our own language, about our own language, are sentences that are undeniable by us. In the above terminology, they are true simpliciter in all possible situations in which the language is ours. They are also such that if you preface them with "Possibly not", the result can be true as well – it is undeniable for me that "cat" is a word for cats, but I must grant that it could have been a word for something else. And it is not undeniable that "cats" was a word for cats in the past, or that it will be in the future. These are simply points that follow from the appreciation of the use/mention distinction, applied to these junctures where the relation of the abstracted semantic term to its pragmatic origin becomes pertinent. In this respect those principles are of course quite different from most ordinary assertions, two ways. First of all, most of our assertions that could not be false, also could not be true when prefaced with "Possibly not" And secondly, most of our assertions are neither infallible nor pragmatic tautologies. That "snow is white" is true, but is not a truism, it is not a pragmatic tautology – it is true because snow is white.[22]

22 I have spelled out the confusions that surround all this in section 9 of PP.

But this discussion of semantic principles, which I take to illuminate what we are to think about truth, seemingly looks as if it is at odds not only with metaphysical realism but with common sense:

> Metaphysical realism "slips from this minimalist sense into substantive postulates". Thus, if we insist "that the structure [in nature] is there independently of any judging, classifying or 'reading' activity", we become the sort of metaphysical realist that van Fraassen opposes. We must not think that "there is in the things classified some real basis for demarcation [...] [and that this] basis must be [...] properties, attributes, Universals, Relations – in short, real structure present in the things".
> Let us again stress what van Fraassen says here: We do not – so van Fraassen's claims – know anything about the real structure of the world. Rather, structure is something we attribute to nature whenever we describe it. (this volume, pp. 86f.)

The reasoning that leads from what I wrote to this bizarre-sounding conclusion must surely hinge on some powerful metaphysical premises!

If I know, as I do, that snow is white, that many apples are red, and that there are nine planets orbiting our sun, does it not follow that I know something about the structure of the world? In saying that these things are true, I attribute structure to the world, but my attributing does not make them true. The meaning of "structure of the world" in the above passage must accordingly be at odds with such a construal – it must be something postulated in the sort of realism about properties, relations, structure in nature, that I reject as needless metaphysical baggage.

I reject (as I explained in my reply to the previous paper) the idea that "the apple is red" cannot be true unless there are abstract things such as redness in addition to the apple. Obviously that does not imply a denial of the truth of such sentences! We can say that we attribute structure to nature whenever we describe something in nature – that is innocuous, if all we mean by "attribute structure" is that we *say that* some things are thus or so, and related to other things in such or such manner. To attribute structure in this sense – which seems quite in order to me – is not to create structure, nor to be the source of structure – it is simply to describe.

So do we know anything at all about the real structure of the world? Not if real structure is meant to be an entity, something like a Universal, a reification of what is predicated. But in that case, no loss. On the other hand, if knowing that there are nine planets in orbits around our sun counts as a case of knowing something about the structure of the world, then we do.

5.3 Making sense of The Scientific Image in retrospect

Having recalled all that about how, at the time I was writing *The Scientific Image*, I was thinking about language, truth, and reference, can I say something more about my nonchalant 'correspondence' terminology there? In general, when we speak, we keep many contextual parameters fixed, and our dialogue partners are alert to what we do in that respect. But in this case, I was unfortunately not signalling to my readers just how blithely I thought we could use abstracted semantic notions as long as they had a clear counterpart in terms of use, users, and contexts. *A theory is true if it corresponds to reality.* Indeed, but that is merely an abstract way of speaking, which has as cash value the instances of form "The statement that there are electrons is true precisely if there are electrons" and the like.

Was I conscious of this? I doubt it. So my initial 'Mea culpa!' was quite in order, and I am glad to have been forced to examine myself, and to tie up, even if belatedly, these loose ends. But now, to the serious challenge, namely that this attitude to the statements using semantic concepts – which regards them as deliberately deficient, so as to serve reasoning by idealization – leads me into murky philosophical waters, where aspiring empiricists can't survive.

> For the constructive empiricist, theories are not about the world. Rather, they are just about the world as it is described by us. Those descriptions, however, do not tell us anything about the real structure of the world – if there is any, that is – because the fact that we attribute structure to nature does not imply that there is any basis in the world that warrants that attribution. Theories that are empirically adequate are true in a tacitly indexical sense. They tell us things we cannot – using our own language – consistently deny. (this volume, p. 89)

By my lights, the first two sentences in this paragraph imply together that there cannot be any such thing as a consistent constructive empiricist. For the two contained sentences

> "Theories are not about the world."
> "Rather, they are just about the world as it is described by us."

contradict each other, in the mouth of any speaker who says them. If a certain description is *my* [*our*] description of something, X, then that is what I am saying it is like. If I say "T is true of X as described in my description, but not true of X" then I am in the first conjunct giving the status of *my description* to something, and denying it that status in the second conjunct – what could be more self-contradictory?[23]

Contrast this with a 3rd person attribution in the neighborhood. Someone could indeed consistently say, for example, "Scientific theories are not about the world. Rather, they are just about the world as it is described by scientists". But note well: this would signal that the speaker (a) considers himself outside the scientific community, and (b) believes that scientific theories are false or vacuous, if taken as descriptions of what they are ostensibly about.

With this point cleared up, can we think that there could possibly be a consistent constructive empiricists after all?

6 There's Life In The Old Dog Yet! – van Fraassen And The Death Of Metaphysics

> "I reject metaphysics, and still I'll say that you exist and that you are a person, a conscious being" (ES, p. 3). In our opinion rejecting metaphysics while still using these concepts would end up in a sort of schizophrenia: Buying traditional metaphysical concepts while claiming that they are part of idle discourse does not seem to result in a comfortable worldview at all. (this volume, p. 100)

23 See further RPS.

Let me begin by saying something nice about metaphysics. After that, I'll address the specific critique that led to the above conclusion.

6.1 The untold riches of metaphysics

In fact I find much to admire in the great metaphysicians of the past. My appreciation is not guided by my allegiances: in the seventeenth century my heroes are Descartes and Leibniz, not Hobbes and Locke. There is a long list of philosophers in our history in whose writings I have found both help and inspiration, and most of what I thus drew on is to be classed as metaphysics. [24]

But the philosophical scene has changed, and what was valuable in their own time I now appreciate because I see it taking on different value. In the seventeenth century there was no boundary line between philosophy and science, I mean not a line that anyone could draw then, though we can draw such lines in retrospect. Because we can draw the lines now, we can distinguish empirical inquiry, theoretical science which remains entirely accountable to empirical inquiry, and theorizing that is not thus accountable in any tangible way. The latter is of course metaphysics, if it is done as a pursuit of factual truth about ourselves and the world we live in, reaching beyond what empirical inquiry can test. But the concepts, theories, and activities falling under that heading today, just as well as the metaphysics of the past, can be drawn on or pursued in another fashion as well.

What I have in mind is an activity that can play some role – I am not sure how great a role – in the overarching hope of philosophy, which is to come to a better understanding of all topics of our concern. In every century we must interpret ourselves to ourselves again, and in every century we have moved far beyond what could be understood in the last century's terms. As part of this we have to ask ourselves about the sciences of our day: how could the world possibly be the way they say it is? To answer this question is to embark on *interpretation.* In general we will understand a theory, like any poem, novel, painting, diary, or chronicle, better if we find still more tenable interpretations and begin to find ways to class other interpretations as untenable

24 I think that I told the story better than I can now in LS, section 3 of the Introduction.

or too forced to provide any insight. The question of truth is not to the point in this enterprise; the prize is understanding. And for this enterprise it has proved very valuable to draw on the concepts and resources fashioned in the great history of metaphysics – sometimes with the result of really making sense even to our contemporary ears, and even more often to bring to light the crucial obscurities that remain after a familiar-sounding story has been poured into the new gourds. As pursuit of greater understanding something that cannot possibly count as a pursuit of truth may yield true bounty still.

But you can see that, if I am right in taking metaphysics to be a pursuit of truth, then this is a break with metaphysics rather than an embrace.

6.2 Does today's metaphysics have a different rationale?

Today's metaphysicians sometimes try to explain themselves as not engaging in a pursuit of truth, claiming to be misunderstood when they are thus depicted as engaged in a sort of armchair science. But several such explanations that I've seen have not borne this out. One is that the metaphysician is simply eliciting all that is implicit in his, her, or our beliefs that we have already. This always reminds me of the Marxist Brunet in Sartre's *Iron in the Soul*:

> 'Schneider', he said without raising his voice, 'It is *conceivable* that [...] the roof of this hut might fall on your head, but that doesn't mean you spend your time keeping a wary eye on the ceiling [...] When you stretch out your hand to grasp your mess-tin, the mere fact of that gesture postulates a universal determinism [...].'

Wonderful how much metaphysics is visibly implicit in our everyday beliefs, to the metaphysicians' eye! But look, *what we believe* is *what we say is true*, and vice versa. Moreover, the eliciting rides not only on pure deductive logic but on demands for explanation – hence is ampliative. So what is this eliciting, but a search for truths not implicitly believed already, but which can supposedly be found in this manner that needs no recourse to observation or experiment?

Similarly for the variant that insists that the metaphysician takes common sense and common experience as starting point, and elicits what the world must have for the common sense to be true and the common experience possible. Anyone who accepts common sense and common experience as veridical, and subscribes to the reasoning involved, will believe, and hence call true, what is thus concluded. So once again we have only been offered a transparent camouflage for the purport to reach truths not uncovered by the empirical sciences.

6.3 Explicanda and simulacra

I complain that in metaphysics we typically see philosophers starting with a genuine problem of human or intellectual interest, but ending up with an understanding of something far removed, something of their own making. In this paper, however, it is suggested that the metaphysician is not so much creating simulacra as *explicanda* of familiar terms or concepts, in the way Carnap outlined. As Carnap pointed out, such *explication* is an activity involved in the empirical sciences as well, and can be of use to the philosopher. He also pointed out, as noted here, that the three criteria of exactness, fruitfulness, and simplicity can compete with each other. The suggestion then continues that my complaint amounts to an insistence on exact matches to the explicata, at the cost of fruitfulness.

Of course I cannot deny that in general explication can advance us in what we want to do, whether in science, in law, or in philosophy. Nor can I insist on priority for exact matching, as if that would be the necessary precondition for such progress, or more specifically for understanding.

The authors of this paper mention first of all examples outside philosophy, in the health sciences, biology, physics, and law. Fine. But where are the examples that show us the fruitfulness of analytic metaphysics? The examples mentioned that can reasonably be ranked under philosophy are the argument from design and from the "suitability of laws of nature" for the existence of God and theodicy – i.e. the problem of pain and evil. These belong to the past; are they really meant as examples of cases where metaphysics led us to a greater understanding?

When I think of examples of contemporary analytic metaphysics, I see just barren ground. For example: after having seen many quite different disquisitions on the part-whole relation, on conditions for some things to be parts of something else, or of these things composing the other thing, and postulates to be added to basic mereology, I had the impression that now every logical nook and cranny had been filled by a real or at least discussed philosophical position, I had a shock. For the range of possible theses had not been exhausted: someone developed the position that nothing has parts, there are only simples arranged in complex spatio-temporal patterns. I thought at first that these would at least have to be very interesting simples! But in fact the only character clearly attributed was that they were simple. Now it would not surprise me if yet another so far unsuspected little logical niche opened up in the field – but it is hard to stay excited ...

6.4 The metaphysical instinct

I began *The Scientific Image* with a quote from Walter Pater, "it is easy to indulge the common metaphysical instinct". Just what is this instinct? It is in part the imperative demand for explanation. This has as its other face the conviction that our own discourse is unintelligible if it lacks a proper metaphysical underpinning. It is this conviction that I see displayed here:

> "I reject metaphysics, and still I'll say that you exist and that you are a person, a conscious being" (ES, p. 3). In our opinion rejecting metaphysics while still using these concepts would end up in a sort of schizophrenia: Buying traditional metaphysical concepts while claiming that they are part of idle discourse does not seem to result in a comfortable worldview at all. (this volume, p. 100)

The authors clearly take it that if I use the concept of person – as I do in much daily discourse – I am already using a metaphysical concept, which would be empty without a metaphysics to which it belongs.

I see no reason to believe that. Metaphysics does not discover foundations needed to give our ordinary discourse ground to stand on, it extrapolates ordinary discourse into airy castles and ramparts in the clouds. Wittgenstein wrote:

> The mathematical problems of what is called foundations are no more the foundations of mathematics for us than the painted rock is the support of the painted tower. (*Remarks on the Foundation of Mathematics*, V, 13).

But the painted rock has a genuine role in the painting that depicts the tower – even that much I cannot say for what analytic metaphysics paints.

7 Laws and Metaphysics – Two Burdens Easily Discarded?

> It seems that van Fraassen drives into a dilemma here. *Either* he insists on eschewing metaphysics – be they modest or ambitious – and gives up his radical rejection of laws of nature. *Or* he accepts a sort of modest metaphysics in his reconstruction of scientific reasoning and will thereby still be able to avoid at least ambitious metaphysics with respect to laws of nature. (this volume, p. 111)

Dilemmas have horns; to find a way between the horns is the most satisfying escape a philosopher can have. While there is philosophizing that I value though it is rightly called metaphysical, the modest metaphysics here held out to me as an option is not of that ilk.[25] This dilemma is not posed here till after an insightful discussion of laws of nature as a problem area in philosophy of science and metaphysics, and I do want to address that. But let me start with the dilemma itself.

7.1 The dilemma and its origin

The dilemma in question derives from what is ostensibly a simple and uncontrovertible point: *to deny the reality of some entity postulated in a metaphysical theory is*

25 Although I said some nice things about metaphysics above, those did not include what I am referring to here. Metaphysics is broad, and certainly includes not only the 'extending empirical science by other means' variety that I reject. But this is not the place to elaborate on this.

to embrace an option in metaphysics – hence to be a metaphysician. For example, to deny the reality of Universals is to be a nominalist, embracing the thesis that there are only concrete individuals. To deny the reality of mental substance is to be a physicalist, and so forth.

Despite these salient examples, I do not think that this point is correct. It seems to me to depend on an assumption about what reasons such a denial can have. If the reason for saying that something does not exist is that the concept in question is incoherent, the denial does not take a contrary metaphysical position about what there is. I deny that there are round square cupolas, that there are massive one-dimensional razor blades, that there are unextended coloured objects, that there is anything red and green all over, that there are distinct sets with the same members, ... In each case, the conjunction of various fairly well understood concepts results in an absurdity, and there is no substantive truth asserted in denying that these results can have any instances.

In serious philosophical disputes, the incoherence cannot be so obvious of course. I deny the reality of sense data, and also the reality of laws of nature. In both cases, I have to specify just which concepts are in play – for unfortunately, different philosophers ostensibly addressing the same topics will use the same words in different senses. It is only a matter of intellectual hygiene to avoid equivocation, either in such denials or in their critique.

The present critique does avoid equivocation, and carefully outlines the different conceptions of law addressed in *Laws and Symmetry*, in Earman's response, and in Swartz' book. If I am to escape between the horns of the posed dilemma, what I have to do is argue that my denial of the reality of laws of nature was based on an incoherence in the *pertinent* concept. But if the escape is to be satisfactory, I should also argue that this concept was not outré, and address the other conceptions to which the writers point us.

7.2 Two ways to understand the idea of laws of nature

Laws of nature are meant to be of nature, but the role they play in discourse in and about science is also crucial to this idea. That role has however been depicted in two ways. One way, which I have always taken to be the one most faithful to its origins as well as to the central role the idea had in modern times before science and philosophy effectively separated, I'll here call

> *the ontological conception*: what the laws of nature are is a fact about nature, as much as the number of planets or the mass of the sun. The history of science cannot affect what laws of nature there are, but the task of science is in part to discover laws of nature.

There is another conception which I see signalled at once in this paper in such passages as

> laws of nature have to be generally true propositions that can be employed to describe facts and to explain processes. (this volume, p. 103)

and is very evident in the summary of Earman's proposal (extending the Mill-Ramsey-Lewis account):

> If the development of science gives rise to the hope of finding a unique theoretical system that gives us a simple and strong description of nature, we should not hesitate to identify the axioms and theorems of this particular system with the laws of nature. (this volume, p. 105)

There are limits to what the history of science can give us by way of theories: the language available to scientists, under any possible conditions, to formulate theories or define families of models can't very well allow those to be indefinable sets of sentences. So these ideas do not fit well with the ontological conception according to which what is possible in the history of science places no limits on what laws of nature there may be. Therefore we must recognize also

> *the epistemic conception*: propositions that express laws of nature are identified by the role they play in science – perhaps science as it shall be in the long run, or science as it would be if developed under ideal conditions of research – and so can only be propositions that can be expressed in forms that can play a role in science.

I do not deny the existence of laws in this sense – I only think there are many open questions concerning this conception, so I will suspend judgement on it for the time being. At least it is not obvious that belief that there are or can be such propositions lands one in metaphysics (any more than talk of e.g. the 'laws of a model').

What I deny is the reality of laws on the ontological conception of what laws of nature are. My denial is not of the sort that takes for granted that this notion makes sense, and opts for a contrary metaphysical position. Instead it is based on an argument to the effect that this conception is incoherent, so that it does not really make sense to ask whether it can have instances at all. So I think that I do after all slip between the horns of the dilemma.

8 Empiricism Without Metaphysics? – On van Fraassen's Conception Of A Stance

> The dilemma I see is this: Rational discourse is only possible as far as the elements of a stance rest ultimately on beliefs or some other equivalent truth-bearing entities; so we conclude that either there is a deep dependence between these other elements and the beliefs, which would be the status of naïve empiricism [...] [o]r you try to solve the connection between beliefs and non-beliefs, on pain of loosing the possibility to argue rationally about the elements under consideration. (this volume, p. 114)

The argument addresses the argument against 'naive empiricism' which I gave in *The Empirical Stance*, and concludes in effect that either my view of empiricism as a stance is vulnerable to the same argument or cannot be subject of rational dispute between philosophers.

In fact the central argument is impeccable, if we grant its premises. A stance is a cluster of attitudes, commitments, values, goals, ... which may include such propositional attitudes as belief, but which cannot as a whole be equated with a belief.[26] My argument against naive empiricism targets any purported empiricist position that satisfies 'Principle ZERO', so that to hold that position is precisely to believe a certain factual thesis. Now the central argument of this paper proceeds in effect:

1 A stance is rationally debatable only if all the attitudes, commitments, values, goals, ... held are based on beliefs.
2 If all the attitudes, commitments, values, goals, ... that compose a stance are based on beliefs, then having that stance amounts to holding a belief.

Both these premises are supported by arguments.

Notice that the central argument does not go through unless in premise 2 we read "based on" in a very strong sense, such that having *what is based on* a belief necessarily implies having that belief. It seems to me that the arguments provided for premise 2 establish at most that beliefs *are involved in* whatever basis one can give for one's attitudes, commitments, etc. But in addition, even when beliefs are the only factors cited as a basis, it does not seem to me that we have a necessary equivalence. This is a familiar point in ethics – if someone else has precisely those beliefs as well, they may not motivate the same attitude or commitment to action. The reason for this is exactly that this other person's values or goals may be different. Even if both agree that something would be best for the welfare of the human race, for example, one person might be so despairing of the witnessed total depravity of this species as to wish its extinction.

It may be countered that some other differences in beliefs will then be present. So the thesis to be examined is: do values, intentions, commitments and the like supervene on beliefs? That is, could someone's values, intentions, etc. be different only if the totality of his or her beliefs would be different too? In the present context this cannot be a psychological question, about what real people are like. So we have to qualify "someone" in some way, as

26 At one point the question is raised whether it matters that the position can be summed up in a single belief. Of course it does not. A set of beliefs held conjointly is not in any relevant way different from a single belief in this context.

e.g. a rational person. In that case, "rational", surely an evaluative term, would also need to be shown to be equatable to a factual description.

This has landed us in a large debate. I won't go further with it, but let me point to two places where there are arguments against this sort of supervenience thesis. One is a series of articles starting with David Lewis's "Desire as belief".[27] The other, which focuses on intention, has Gilbert Harman's 'Practical Reasoning' as a representative example.[28]

But the much more important question raised for me concerns the first premise. The arguments for it present a strong argument against my view. They start in section 3. With

> how is one supposed to decide between different, mutually excluding philosophical theories as stances? Van Fraassen seems to have two different replies to this challenge. (this volume, pp. 116f.)

The first reply cited from the 2004 symposium on the book is that those who have different stances can argue on the basis of shared or common values. Perhaps that is the simple case; and the range of argument will clearly be limited by just how much is shared. For the areas in which distinctly different values are held, I claimed that it is possible to respectfully acknowledge someone else's values without giving up one's own, thus also still allowing for possibly effective dialogue.

This first reply still makes sense even if the above premise 1. is accepted. The sharing of values would in that case derive from shared beliefs; and it is common place that a discussion of differences in belief must and can start from a basis of shared belief. But not accepting that premise I am naturally led to what is here cited as second response: the claim that there can be rational disagreement and discourse even outside the sphere of belief. This presupposes, certainly, that values are not simply personal or communal 'bare' preferences, so that all one would be able to say is *de gustibus non disputandum.*

27 Lewis (1982). John Collins presents an argument against a non-quantitative version of the Thesis in Collins (1988) and Lewis' argument was simplified and strengthened by Horacio Arlo Costa, John Collins, and Isaac Levi in Arlo Costa et. al. (1995).

28 See further Ch. 8 of Harman (1986). For extensive discussion of this and related literature see Speaks (2004).

This is certainly a subject that can be and is discussed abstractly and in great generality. But perhaps here it is more convincing to think of the relevant examples in the empiricist critique of analytic metaphysics. A demand is not a belief – and neither is the status of the demand for explanation between empiricist and metaphysician. Certainly a value judgement is involved, concerning the extent to which explanation is to be prized in the formation of a philosophical position or account. It has seemed to me that simply bringing to light how strong, far-reaching, and general this demand is in the practice of metaphysics will have an effect. The metaphysician will not, by his own lights, consider it right then to ignore the question of limits to this demand. I can illustrate how it can lead to requirements on e.g. scientific theorizing if it is pressed very far, which are not accepted within science.

Of course, I needed to correctly discern something about the values active in the metaphysicians' practice, if I were to come up with a point to which they could not automatically respond with "So what?". That something did not need to be a value I shared – just something that would make my raising the point about explanation *motivating* for a metaphysical partner in dialogue. To be partners in this sense, in turn, requires that we acknowledge each other's positions with sufficient respect for the dialogue to continue.

It is true that there is no guarantee that philosophers of different stripes, even within the context of the Western philosophical canon, will converge to a common point in this sort of mutually stimulated evolution. But does that not apply equally well even if all differences are differences in belief? Each partner can bring more of the other's presuppositions to light, and attempt to adduce more evidence so as to provide more of a shared basis. There is no guarantee that in such a dialogue the views will converge to a common point – at least not without strong assumptions about a shared range of conceptual options. In this respect dialogue between different stances seems to me to be in no worse position than dialogue between different factual beliefs, at least in philosophy, where the practice is not so strongly rule or paradigm governed as perhaps it is in some other forms of life. If that is granted, then we can maintain the offered view of philosophical positions as stances rather than beliefs.

REFERENCES

Arlo-Costa, Horacio, John Collins, and Isaac Levi (1995): "Desire as Belief Implies Opinionation or Indifference", *Analysis*, 55.1 (January 1995), pp. 2-5.

Armstrong, David (19983): *What is a Law of Nature?* Cambridge: Cambridge University Press.

Collins, John (1988): "Belief, Desire, and Revision", *Mind* 97 (1988) pp. 333-342.

Dancy, Jonathan (2004): *Ethics Without Principles.* Oxford: Oxford University Press.

Muller, Fred (2005): "The Deep Black Sea: Observability and Modality Afloat", *British Journal for the Philosophy of Science* 56 (2005), pp. 61-99.

Harman, Gilbert (1976): "Practical Reasoning", *Review of Metaphysics* 79 (1976), pp. 431-463.

Harman, Gilbert (1986): *Change in View.* Cambridge, MA: MIT Press.

Holton Richard (1994): "Deciding To Trust, Coming To Believe", *Australasian Journal of Philosophy* 72-1 (1994), pp. 63-76.

Lewis, David (1988): "Desire as Belief" *Mind* 97 (1988), pp. 323-33.

Lipton, Peter (2004): *Inference to the Best Explanation.* 2nd ed. London: Routledge.

Putnam, Hilary (1975): *Mathematics, Matter and Method.* Cambridge: Cambridge University Press.

Seager, William (1988): "Scientific Anti-realism and the Epistemic Community", *PSA* 1988, vol. 1, pp. 181-187.

Speaks, Jeff (2004): "Belief, Intention, Intentional Action, and the Simple View" at http://www.arts.mcgill.ca/philo/speaks/519-action/bratman-belief-intention.html

Worrall, John (1989): "Structural realism: the best of both worlds?", *Dialectica* 43 (1989), pp. 99-124.

CPSIA information can be obtained
at www.ICGtesting.com
Printed in the USA
LVIC05n2239200115
423660LV00004B/16

* 9 7 8 3 1 1 0 3 2 5 3 2 4 *